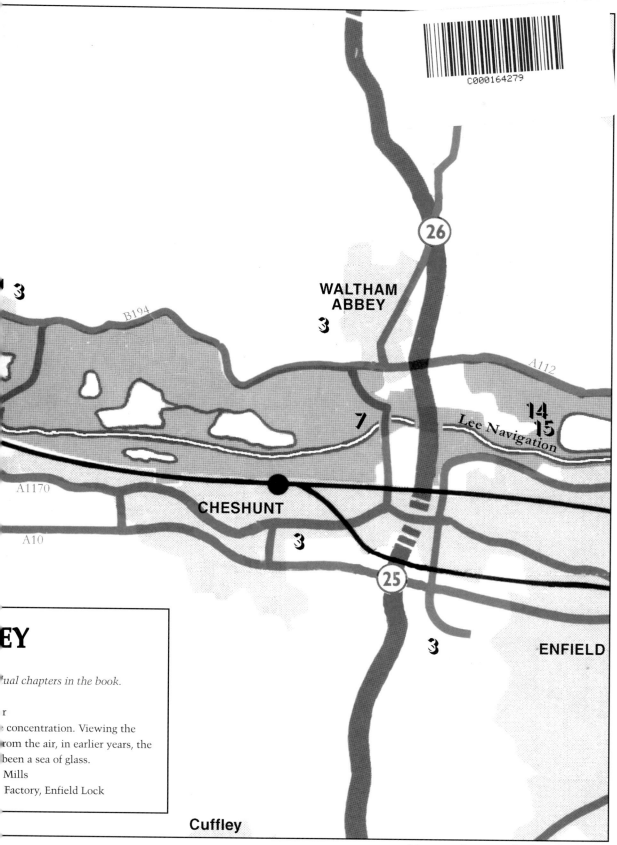

WALTHAM
ABBEY

B194

A112

Lee Navigation

14
15

7

A1170

CHESHUNT

A10

26

25

ENFIELD

EY

ual chapters in the book.

r

concentration. Viewing the
rom the air, in earlier years, the
been a sea of glass.
Mills
Factory, Enfield Lock

Cuffley

Map continues on back endpaper ➔

London's
LEA VALLEY

Britain's Best Kept Secret

London's
LEA VALLEY

Britain's Best Kept Secret

Jim Lewis

Phillimore

1999

Published by
PHILLIMORE & CO. LTD.
Shopwyke Manor Barn, Chichester, West Sussex

ISBN 1 86077 100 9

Printed and bound in Great Britain by
BOOKCRAFT LTD.
Midsomer Norton

This book is dedicated to my wife, companion and editor, Jenny, without whom it is doubtful if this work could ever have been completed.

Contents

The author Dr. Jim Lewis with former Chairman and Managing Director of Thorn EMI Ferguson, Richard E. (Dickie) Norman CBE. The picture shows the unveiling of a history board on the site of the former Thorn EMI Ferguson laboratory and factory, where a supermarket now stands. (Photograph reproduced with permission of Tony Saunders, Middlesex University Press Office.)

Foreword

Mike Nixon—Chief Executive North London Training &
Enterprise Council and Business Link.

THIS BOOK recognises, for the first time, the uniqueness of the Lea Valley as the birthplace of the post-industrial revolution. It also highlights the outstanding contribution made by its entrepreneurs and workforce, over a period of more than 200 years, to a diverse range of products and technical achievements. This entrepreneurial spirit lives on in North London, monitored and supported by The North London Training & Enterprise Council and Business Link.

While the Lea Valley, in recent years, has suffered from changes in global economy, in his conclusion, Dr. Lewis has pointed to a number of encouraging indicators which signal a bright social and economic future for the region.

Mike Nixon

Acknowledgements

THE AUTHOR wishes to thank the following organisations, companies and societies for their encouragement, support and advice and for supplying many of the illustrations within this book:

Alexandra Palace and Park Trust, Wood Green, London
Alexandra Palace Television Trust, Wood Green, London
BOC Process Plants, Edmonton, London
Bruce Castle Museum, Tottenham, London
Caradon MK Limited, Basildon, Essex
Civix, Old Street, London
Edmonton Hundred Historical Society, Enfield, Middlesex
Enfield Business Centre, Hertford Road, Enfield
Enfield Enterprise Agency, Hertford Road, Enfield
Enfield Local History Section, Southgate Town Hall, London
Ford Motor Company, Ponders End, Enfield
Gestetner Limited, Shoreditch, London
G R Wright & Sons Limited, Ponders End, Enfield
Gunpowder Mills Study Group, Guildford, Surrey
Hawker Siddeley Power Transformers, Walthamstow, London
Hornsey Historical Society, Hornsey, London
Johnson Matthey, Brimsdown, Enfield
Lee Valley Business and Innovation Centre, Innover Park, Enfield
Lee Valley Regional Park Authority, Myddelton House, Enfield
London Borough of Enfield, Civic Centre, Enfield
London Borough of Haringey, Civic Centre, Haringey
Marx Memorial Library, Islington, London
Merk Sharp & Dome, Ponders End, Enfield
Ministry of Defence Pattern Room, Nottingham
Newham Local History Library, Newham, London
North London TEC Limited, Palmers Green, London
Northern Telecom, New Southgate, London
Phillips Auctioneers & Valuers, New Bond Street, London
River Lea Tidal Mill Trust, Bromley by Bow, London
Southgate District Civic Trust, Southgate, London
Thames Water, Walthamstow, London

The British Vintage Wireless Society, Tottenham, London
The Great Eastern Railway Society, North Woolwich, London
The Greater London Record Office, Northampton Road, London
The Hackney Society, Eleanor Road, Hackney, London
The House of Lords Record Office, Westminster, London
The Institution of Electrical Engineers, Savoy Place, London
The Institution of Incorporated Engineers, Savoy Hill, London
The Institution of Civil Engineers, George Street, London
The Institution of Mechanical Engineers, Birdcage Walk, London
The Jewish Museum, Finchley, London
The Lea Valley Growers' Association, Cheshunt, Hertfordshire
The London Gas Museum, Bromley-by-Bow, London
The National Army Museum, Chelsea, London
The National Maritime Museum, Greenwich, London
The New River Action Group, Hornsey, London
The Public Record Office, Kew, Richmond, Surrey
The Royal Society of Chemistry, Burlington House, London
The Royal Television Society, Holborn Hall, London
The Science Museum, Kensington, London
The Thorn EMI Archive, Hayes, Middlesex
The Wallaceburg and District Museum, Wallaceburg, Ontario, Canada
Thermos Limited, Brentwood, Essex
Tower Hamlets Local History Library, Tower Hamlets, London
Vestry House Museum, Walthamstow, London

While many individuals have freely given their knowledge, some unknowingly, which has contributed greatly to the production of this book, I must pay a special tribute to my very good friend Dr. Fred Clark, who, like the author, has a passion for discovering the industrial heritage of the Lea Valley.

Introduction

ASK ANY self respecting history student where the Industrial Revolution began you and will probably get the correct answer. However, ask the question where was the birthplace of the post-industrial revolution—the technological revolution—and the inquirer is likely to be met with a blank stare. In fact ask the question of the majority of people living within the vicinity of North or East London and you are sure to receive a similar response. The answer, of course, is the Lea Valley, or more precisely, Ponders End, Enfield.

I suspect, as with many people who have worked and lived in the Lea Valley, I shared a vague awareness of some of the past industrial achievements and technological triumphs without giving too much thought to the benefits which the region had brought to the world. However, it was not until I began to research into projects aimed at creating social and economic regeneration within the region that the Valley began to offer up its secrets. The experience of these discoveries, which still occur regularly and seem to be almost endless, cannot be understated. I would liken these discoveries to the opening of a vast treasure chest which, in the case of the Lea Valley, appears to have a dimension of infinite depth.

In this book we begin to explore the lives, inventions and discoveries of the many famous and fascinating people who, over a period of almost two hundred years, unknowingly created a region of Britain which, for its compact geographical size, stands unrivalled in the history of technology. From the many examples of discovery, invention and entrepreneurship, there emerges a story of inward and outward technology transfer—in modern parlance 'spin out' and 'spin in'—which has helped to mould and shape the world in which we live today.

When considering the format for this book, which has been based on a number of previously published articles, it was felt that the object of the exercise was three-fold.

Firstly, it was important to begin recording and highlighting the regional achievements.

Secondly, it was thought necessary to draw people's attention to the fact that, over the years, the Lea Valley workforce had contributed greatly to the region's technological achievements and that the inventiveness, skill and entrepreneurship had remained ingrained in the succeeding generations, almost like a strand of DNA. And, thirdly, it was felt that by drawing the reader's attention to the rich industrial heritage of the region in a more general way, rather than giving each of the separate subjects an in-depth treatment, the book would have wider appeal. By adopting this approach it is hoped to encourage not only the casual reader but also the serious student to undertake further research and to uncover more of the region's technological secrets. Therefore, I apologise in advance to those who had wished to see a fuller treatment of a particular industry, technology or person.

Throughout the book opportunities for research will be provided through the introduction of people who subsequently became famous, although little is known of their lives during the time they lived or worked in the Lea Valley.

While the aim of this book is to remind the reader of the Lea Valley's technological heritage, prior to the rapid decline which began in the 1970s, it would be inappropriate not to mention the new strategies being introduced by the British Government and the European Union to promote the long-term social and economic regeneration of the region. The opportunity will be taken to explain briefly these new initiatives and to show how a fresh approach through partnership between Europe, Local Authorities, UK Government, Lee Valley Regional Park Authority, educational establishments, industry, commerce and the various support agencies, together with the local community, will once again create a Lea Valley of which to be proud.

Note: Throughout this book the convention of spelling 'Lea' when referring to the River and 'Lee' in relation to the Navigation will be adhered to.

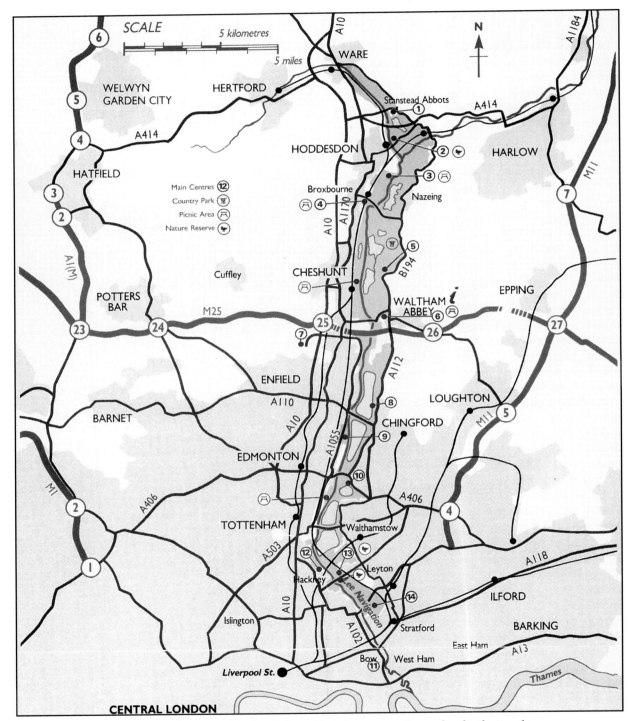

Map showing the region of the Lea Valley with its interconnecting road and rail networks.

The Lea Valley

THE SPELLING of Lea or Lee has been a controversial issue for many years. When writing articles for local newspapers on the subject, one is likely to receive a considerable emotional response from the public. Some correspondents become quite dogmatic, insisting that only their particular choice of spelling is correct.

However, when addressing local telephone directories it will soon become apparent that the spelling 'Lea' in company headings outnumbers 'Lee' by almost four to one. Consulting maps of the region can be equally unhelpful as both spellings for the river can be found. In some instances the spelling refers to the river as Lea, while the canalised navigation is spelt Lee. So which is correct?

Perhaps the problem can be solved by consulting early legislation in the two River Improvement Acts of 1424 and 1430. Here the spelling was 'Ley'. In a later Act of 1571, which was greatly to improve the river as a major transport link between London and the hinterland, the spelling adopted was the 'Ryver of Lee' or the 'Ryver of Lee otherwise called Ware Ryver'. At the time the town of Ware was an important inland port.

Dr. Keith Fairclough, who has carried out extensive research into the history of the river, has discovered in Elizabethan documents that all three spellings, Lee, Lea and Ley were used, although Lee was the most frequent. He explains:

when discussion turns to the body of trustees first appointed in 1739 or the canalised navigation that was introduced in 1767, the spelling Lee must be adopted, because that is how they were first officially spelt in the enabling acts of

The Lee Navigation at Enfield Lock with Government Row, the houses built for the former RSAF workers c.1815, in the background.

parliament, and because that is how they have always been spelt subsequently in official documents. Thus it must always be the Lee Navigation, even though it could be either the river Lea or the river Lee.

I am sure Dr. Fairclough's rational explanation clears up once and for all the confused spelling!

For almost one thousand years, the Lea Valley has been responsible for sustaining successive generations, providing the essentials of life, food and work. The Valley, although a shadow of its former industrial self, still plays an important part in the health of London, producing drinking water for the capital through a complex of reservoirs, filter beds and pumping

1

Fishermen just south of Ponders End Lock with the Ford Motor Company factory in the background.

Swans on the River Lea above Waltham Abbey.

stations and the natural resources of Epping Forest on the eastern slopes act as a lung, supplying fresh air.

For several hundred years, the River Lea supplied power for milling grain along its length, from its source in Bedfordshire to the point where it joins the Thames at Bow Creek, allowing the bakeries of the metropolis to provide the citizens with their daily bread. As a vital link between the capital and the hinterland, the Lea provided not only the means of transport for produce and materials to the markets and manufacturers of the region, but power to the growing industries.

Glimpses of Britain's industrial heritage can be seen by walking or cycling along the Lee tow path. Here, much evidence can be found of the manufacturing history that put the 'Great' into Great Britain.

The Lea Valley was home to a profusion of diverse and important industries, amongst others the design and manufacture of ships, boats, explosives, armaments, porcelain, bricks, perfume, chemicals, plastics, furniture, floor and wall coverings, vehicles and their accessories, rubber commodities, footware, clothes, alcoholic beverages, musical instruments, office equipment, electronic and electrical goods: the list appears endless.

Alas, the tragic loss of Lea Valley industries in recent years has been influenced by shifts in the world's manufacturing base. The region has been classified by the European Union as a socially and economically deprived area and granted Objective 2 status. This means that European funds have been made available for projects which will initiate the social and economic regeneration of the area. It is hoped, through these measures, that the Lea Valley will once more become a vibrant economic region, although it is recognised that its former industrial might cannot be fully reinstated.

However, by the introduction of new technologies and the development of tourism and leisure facilities (some of the proposed initiatives are based upon the educational aspects of the region's rich industrial heritage) the Lea Valley looks set, once again, to provide the essentials of life as we enter the new millennium.

REFERENCES

Fairclough, Keith, 'Leaway or Licence?', *Catalyst*, issue no.2 (Middlesex University, March 1995)

An imaginative scheme to bring fresh drinking water to the City of London, a distance of approximately twenty miles from the springs situated north of the metropolis at Amwell and Chadwell in Hertfordshire, began on 21 April 1609. After several Acts of Parliament concerned with bringing water to London and a rather dilatory approach to such schemes by the Corporation (progress was apparently hindered by high cost), a proposal put forward by Hugh Myddleton (later Sir) to fund and manage the venture was accepted formally (perhaps enthusiastically) on 28 March 1609.

Myddleton was born at Galch Hill near Denbigh, in or about the year 1555. He came from a large family of nine brothers and seven sisters. His father Richard, who had been Governor of Denbigh Castle, died in 1575. His mother Jane had departed this life some ten years earlier in 1565. Hugh started his working career apprenticed to the Goldsmiths' Company and it would seem that part of his employment included banking and money-changing. Between the years 1603 and 1628, he had been returned as Member of Parliament for the Borough of Denbigh on six occasions. It is probably fair to say that, had Hugh lived today, he would be labelled a venture capitalist and risk taker.

The plan for the construction of the New River, as it became known, was to follow closely the 100-foot contour along the western slopes of the Lea Valley, the destination being a storage pond or reservoir to be dug at Islington. By deciding this route for the River, it effectively doubled the distance the water had to travel from twenty to almost forty miles. However, what is

Sir Hugh Myddleton who, with King James I, put up the money to construct the New River.

so staggering about this project, which must be seen in the context of the day as a considerable feat of engineering, is that the channel dug from Hertfordshire brought water to the City by gravity only. The average fall of water to Islington was only 5½ inches (14cm) per mile. In Britain, at that time, the use of pumps for shifting water was relatively rare.

Although construction of the New River was held up for almost two years due to disputes with landowners over compensation, the work was completed when the course was extended to Islington in April 1613. The official opening ceremony took place on 29 September that year with much celebration. When we consider the problems which had to be overcome, the speed of the waterway's completion is truly remarkable. It is recorded that 157 bridges spanned the river, which generally flowed north to south. However, there were many streams to negotiate which ran west to east across the valley carrying land drainage water. To reduce the risk of

Broadmead Pumping Station, constructed 1880, on the New River at Ware in Hertfordshire. The building is Grade II listed and modern electric pumps now lift the water from the aquifer to recharge the river.

contamination to the clean water in the New River, these streams were allowed to follow their natural course towards the River Lea by being taken beneath the line of the new channel.

When the New River was dug Islington was effectively a village set in open country and situated approximately one hundred feet above the level of the Thames. The spot for the storage pond was deliberately chosen to take advantage of the natural fall of the land towards the City. This made water distribution relatively easy and it was possible, under gravity, to pipe water to the height of the second floor of some houses.

By today's standards water distribution was rather crude. The main conduits were positioned above ground, sometimes on trestles, and were constructed from drilled sections of elm tree trunks. Each section was joined to the next by creating a friction joint secured with an iron ring. One end of a section was made to fit the next by shaping the mating piece like the sharpened end of a pencil. Individual house supplies were taken from the wooden main via a small bore lead pipe which was usually terminated with a swan-necked cock for drawing off the water.

While those who benefited from this new method of water distribution were no doubt overjoyed, the system was very inefficient. Early in the 19th century it was reported that there were losses from the supply of 25 per cent, attributed to leaks from pipes alone. However, it would be unwise to be too critical, considering the primitive nature of this early technology, as it has been reported only recently that losses of water from leaking pipes in some regions of Britain have been as high as 40 percent.

As the population of London increased, so did the demand for fresh drinking water. Over the years the New River saw many modifications to increase and quicken the flow into London. Bends were straightened, wells were dug, reservoirs were built and pumps installed. Today, when trying to trace the original route of the New River, it will be noticed that much has been filled in. However, due to sustained pressure

The New Gauge feeding water from the River Lea into the New River.

White House Sluice on the New River at Ware, Hertfordshire.

The Marble Gauge, erected in 1770, which formerly controlled the amount of water from the Manifold Ditch (the former course of the River Lea) to the New River.

The view to Alexandra Palace across the filter beds at the Hornsey Pumping Station on the New River in north London.

from environmentally conscious community groups a considerable amount of this ancient waterway has been saved.

Today, some of the remaining sections of the New River form an integral and important part of a much larger and complex system of reservoirs, treatment works, pumping stations and filter beds stretching along much of the length of the Lea Valley. Recently a scheme was completed to take water from the New River to re-charge the region's depleted aquifer, effectively connecting the ancient artefact to Thames Water's state-of-the-art London Ring Main which tunnels through clay 40 metres below the metropolis. Incidentally, the depth of the Ring Main was chosen to avoid interference with the London Transport Underground system.

Who could have imagined that almost four hundred years after the completion of the New River, the citizens of London would still be deriving benefit from the water, brought to them by the remarkable skill and achievements of those early engineers and surveyors who designed and planned the waterway? Also we should not forget the contribution made by the labourers, who through hard manual toil shifted hundreds of tons of earth in digging the course of the river.

REFERENCES

Author unknown, *London's Water Supply in the 21st Century: A strategy for water treatment and trunk distribution* (Thames Water, February 1986)

Harwood, Elain, *The New River* (report by English Heritage, August 1989)

Morris, R.E., *History of the New River*, 1934

The Valley that Fed the Metropolis

NO BOOK about the Lea Valley would be complete without mentioning the role of the glasshouse industry, which began to put down its early roots in the upper part of the valley towards the end of the 19th century. Before this, there were several nurseries and market gardens in the lower part of the Lea Valley. Some of the earliest can be traced back to the 17th century, in areas such as Hackney, Clapton, Tottenham, Walthamstow and Edmonton.

The Lea Valley would seem to have been an ideal choice for those early growers wishing to establish their industry. Well drained fertile loams and a plentiful water supply, from rivers and wells, were spread throughout the region. The navigable River Lea, which linked directly to the River Thames and the capital's network of canals, provided direct access for goods and produce to the markets of London. As the developing metropolis began its inevitable expansion in the Victorian and early Edwardian era, the lower part of the Lea Valley not only provided the space for the industrial move out of the capital, but also the much needed land for workers' houses.

With the railway spreading its tracks northwards up the Lea Valley and with industry and housing clamouring for space in the lower regions, the relatively undeveloped nursery land in the south became an obvious target for the developers. With the southern nursery land becoming a desirable commodity and the increasing amount of atmospheric pollution from the re-located factories, many growers came under pressure to move further northward along the valley to where the air was cleaner and the land cheaper. Gradually growers re-located their businesses and erected their glasshouses on open land in suburbs such as Enfield, Cheshunt, Nazeing and Waltham Abbey.

Peter Rooke, whose grandfather George set up in business as a Lea Valley nurseryman in the 1880s, suggests that the early 19th-century nurseries 'were little more than areas of ground where vegetables and garden bedding plants were grown in open air for the market'. However, later in the century this changed with the development of the commercial greenhouse, encouraged, in 1845, by the removal of tax on sheet glass and improvements in heating and ventilation systems. By the 1930s, it is claimed, the Lea Valley had the world's largest concentration of greenhouses, with the Hertfordshire sector alone producing half of Britain's total horticultural output. This was now a major industry producing a wide variety of crops, with bulk supplies of tomatoes and cucumbers providing a cheap food source for the markets of Britain.

A view from the air, c.1960, of the concentration of glass houses at Cheshunt.

Many industries, particularly the motor manufacturers who established themselves around Birmingham, encouraged providers of parts and services to set up in business nearby to provide a support infrastructure. The Lea Valley growers were no exception. In Tottenham alone there were several manufacturers and distributors of greenhouses, Duncan Tucker of Lawrence Road being one of the largest. Samuel South and Sons, of White Hart Lane, Tottenham, was a major supplier of a variety of clay flower pots to the industry. This company manufactured its pots on site, having its own clay pits, kilns

A workman with contrasting size flower pots at Messrs South of White Hart Lane, Tottenham, c.1927.

and drying sheds.

By the start of the Great War the Lea Valley growers were developing into a major, and necessary, industry. This was recognised by government, when in 1915, to support the growers, a Research and Experimental Station was set up at Cheshunt by the Ministry of Agriculture. However, in the years succeeding the Second World War, as in other areas of manufacturing, the Lea Valley horticultural industry began to come under increasing pressure from overseas growers able to produce certain crops more cheaply. Initially the Lea Valley growers maintained an advantage over cheap imports into the UK, as the cost of transporting this type of produce, which was essentially perishable, was still prohibitive.

General view of a block of cucumber houses, each 225 feet long by 15 feet wide which once stood on a site near Waltham Cross, Hertfordshire.

With advances in technology, such as refrigerated vehicles and faster and larger aircraft, it became possible to have fruit and vegetables brought in from destinations never before considered a threat, often within twenty-four hours of harvesting, for sale in the British markets. Many of these overseas growers, unlike their counterparts in the Lea Valley, were not constrained by the vagaries of the British climate which could saddle the UK grower with high heating bills. Even a switch from coal-fired heating to the cheaper and more efficient oil-fired systems in the 1950s could not prevent many growers from leaving the industry eventually. When this happened, the land on which the nurseries had stood was usually sold for building the swathe of new housing, to accommodate, in many cases, the workers who had moved out of London to follow their respective industries further up the valley.

Now the Lea Valley horticultural industry, which includes both edible and ornamental produce (flowers), is only approximately 300 acres in area. In the 1950s, the figure was 1,300 acres. However, with the help of new technology and improved growing techniques, crop yields,

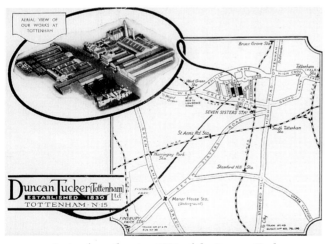

A view from the air, c.1936, of the Duncan Tucker factory at Lawrence Road, Tottenham (established 1830). Later and up until the 1980s, Thorn Lighting had a factory on this site.

particularly those under glass, have increased dramatically. For example, in the mid-1970s the yield for tomatoes was around seventy tons per acre; today the figure is an astonishing 250 tons. Cucumber production has also become more efficient with the Lea Valley growers producing one third of the nation's output.

Once, the Lea Valley's produce was directed towards the traditional markets of London, in particular Covent Garden and Spitalfields, with the individual growers being responsible for grading, packing and transport. Now, due mainly to changes in the buying habits of the public, independent houses arrange the handling, grading and packing, with the support of computerised systems, before shipping the produce direct to the major supermarket chains. Often these retailers contract to purchase the entire output of a single grower. As may be imagined, these new ways of working are achieved with a fraction of the labour force formerly employed.

Major changes have also taken place within the house and bedding plant side of the industry, particularly in the areas of sales, marketing and production. The demise of internationally respected growers like Thomas Rochford at Turnford has left a gap in this sector of the market. With increasing public interest in gardening, brought about, in the main, by popular television programmes and magazines on the subject, the Lea Valley growers have yet again

responded to the challenge. Concentrated in areas such as Crews Hill, Enfield and elsewhere in the valley there is now a substantial garden centre industry.

In localities like Crews Hill relatively little growing takes place, although there is some preparation and production of bedding plant packs for the increasingly popular superstore-type garden centres. The grouping of nurseries and garden centres in one place has resulted in a major attraction for the aspiring and serious gardener. Here the public are invited to buy not only plants direct from the suppliers, but also a staggering range of equipment. This includes garden ornaments, furniture, lighting, fencing, tools, sheds, paving, ponds and, not surprisingly, greenhouses.

While external pressures have brought many changes to the shape and structure of the Lea Valley glasshouse industry, the growers, supported by their own Association, have always shown considerable resilience and ingenuity in the fight for survival. This has been particularly true in the face of cheap produce arriving from abroad from countries with lower labour costs and better climatic conditions than the UK.

A mark of the industry's resilience can be seen in the post-war period of the 1950s when it was difficult for the Lea Valley growers to attract and retain labour. Workers, at the time, were being enticed from horticulture to higher paid jobs on offer from the manufacturing industries located a short distance away down the Lea Valley. To counteract this trend, experienced workers were encouraged to come from Sicily and Italy to fill the vacancies. Several of these people worked extremely hard in their new country and in a relatively short time started businesses on their own account, or took over existing nurseries.

The success of the immigrant community was such that by the late 1970s over 50 per cent of the Lea Valley growers were Italian, and, with a further nine per cent of businesses being run by people coming from other countries, the British grower was now in the minority. However, it might be fair to speculate that without the intervention and support of the immigrant growers in the 1950s and 1960s, it is doubtful if the Lea Valley glasshouse industry would have developed into the competitive and efficient industry which we see today.

REFERENCES

Author unknown, *Golden Jubilee of the Lea Valley Growers' Association—October 1911-October 1961* (National Farmers Union, Hertfordshire, 1961)

Currie, C.R.J. (ed.), *The Victoria History of the County of Middlesex—Hackney Parish*, vol.10 (University of London Press, 1995)

Rooke, Peter, 'The Lea Valley Nursery Industry', *Hertfordshire's Past*, no.42 (Hertfordshire Archaeological Council, Autumn 1997)

Stevenson, R.A. (Tony), Lea Valley Growers' Association, private conversation and correspondence, June/July 1998

Flour Power in the Lea Valley

IN 1867 George Reynolds Wright came to Enfield and entered into partnership with James Dilly Young, the miller of Ponders End Mill, taking up residence in the East Mill House. The house, built in the reign of Queen Anne, is in active use today providing the necessary accommodation to administer the only independent family-run flour mill in London. Speaking to directors and staff of this company will immediately reveal a love and enthusiasm for a proud tradition of milling at Ponders End, whose roots can be traced back as far as Domesday Book.

George Reynolds Wright (1824-1914) founder of Wright's Mill at Ponders End.

By the early years of the 17th century the mill was known as Flanders Mill. Power to drive the seven pairs of millstones came from the River Lea via two breast water wheels. Evidence of this earlier water power can still be observed today. If a visitor stands on the bridge, which is part of the Lea Valley Road running between the King George and William Girling reservoirs, and

looks north, a weir will be seen which allows water from the river to enter the mill head stream that passes directly below them. In the 18th century the mill became known as Enfield Mill, changing its name again halfway through the 19th century to Ponders End Mill.

In the early days of milling, flour had to be delivered to the bakeries of London and the surrounding area by horse-drawn wagon. A typical day for the carman would start around 6a.m. when he would leave the mill with a full load of five tons, ensuring the route he took did not have too many steep and difficult slopes. After a round trip of some ten to twenty miles he would return about 7p.m., not finishing the day until his main asset, the horses, had been fed, watered and stabled. Next day, an appointed operative would come to work early in the morning to see that the horses were harnessed and ready for the day's deliveries.

By 1909 the new technology of electricity had become the energy source and traditional methods of powering the mill—water and steam—were abandoned. This also gave the opportunity to replace the ageing millstones, which required regular maintenance and dressing by skilled craftsmen, with modern efficient roller machinery which, at the time, was being introduced almost universally by the milling industry. However, up until the 1960s some of the millstones were retained by Wright's, who were committed to maintaining a service to a number of their customers who required specialist flour.

The early 20th century also brought with it an improved road network and in August 1906 the Company took advantage of this by acquiring a steam wagon. This dramatically increased the amount of flour which could be transported compared with the horse-drawn wagon. However, steam wagons of the day had certain drawbacks. Initially these vehicles had solid iron wheels which caused considerable problems for their drivers when descending or ascending hills with bulk loads of between fifteen and twenty

Oldest known picture of Wright's Mill c.1880.

tons, particularly when the roads were icy or wet.

Those were hard times for our ancestors but we can be proud of their achievements which have helped successive generations of Wrights to invest confidently in the future of the mill, preserving part of the Lea Valley's rich industrial heritage.

The year 1938 saw a significant leap forward in the fortunes of the mill when the directors, no doubt with expansion firmly in mind, purchased, from the Metropolitan Water Board, freehold ownership of a little over eleven acres of surrounding land and the entitlement of passage for barges from and to the Lee Navigation.

When the Second World War commenced in 1939 the mill came under Government control. To help secure food supplies for the nation, and to supplement the losses caused by the bombing of the mills situated in the London Docks, the production at Ponders End was considerably increased. This was achieved by extending the working of the mill to seven days a week and 52 weeks a year for the duration of the war. Fortunately the mill did not suffer any serious damage from enemy action, although constant operation of the plant took its toll on the machinery.

By the early 1950s, with the mill back in family control, a decision was taken to modernise and refurbish the plant and machinery. The specialist firm of Thomas Robinson of Rochdale was called in and by April that year, only 10 weeks after modernisation began, the mill recommenced production with a 50 per cent increase in capacity. Flour could now be processed at the rate of twelve 280lb sacks per hour.

Company expansion still continues towards the millennium and beyond with improvements in buildings and equipment and the introduction of silos for bulk storage of grain and flour. Modern methods of production call for changes to the way in which flour is transported, so Wright's have invested in bulk road tankers. No

Wheat arriving at Wright's Mill by barge on the River Lea c.1955.

doubt the 19th-century wagon driver would have found these new methods of storage and delivery impossible to imagine.

Not resting on their laurels, the directors of Wright's have responded to changing public tastes, by introducing a number of new product lines particularly aimed at today's busy consumer. Speciality flours and bread mixes, which can be made quickly and easily, now appear on several supermarket shelves and expansion into overseas markets is an ongoing feature of the business strategy.

Over the years many Lea Valley companies have come and gone, but Wright's Mill stands as a glowing example of determination and entrepreneurship, a symbol of the ability of a family business to adapt product and processes to the needs of a highly competitive and ever changing industrial world.

Women workers on the pre-pack line at Wright's Mill c.1948.

The example of progression from Wright's early Lea Valley roots and the company's successful expansion into the 20th century must surely act not only as encouragement to other firms wishing to set up in the region, but as a continuing reminder of how to adapt and prosper. Here are important lessons for us all to learn and perhaps the Wright model can supply some valuable clues for industry in general, pointing the way to future regeneration of the region.

REFERENCES

G.R. Wright & Sons Limited, *The Story of a Family Business* (undated brochure)

Interview with Mr. David Wright, the current Chairman of G.R. Wright & Sons Limited.

Note: Mr. David Wright is the fifth generation of the family involved with milling at Ponders End since his ancestor entered the business in the 1860s. Fortunately there is a sixth generation of Wrights maturing in the wings.

The Lea Valley and the State of Israel

STRANGE as it may seem, Three Mills, situated at the foot of the Lea Valley in the London Borough of Newham, at Bromley by Bow, has a direct link with the State of Israel. The history of the site can be traced back to at least the 11th century, when it was recorded in Domesday Book that there were nine mills in existence, though the link with Israel was not forged until the 20th century.

In the early part of this century a young biochemist left his native Russia for England, first taking up a university teaching and research post in Manchester. Apart from his academic career, he was passionately committed to Zionism, working tirelessly to establish a homeland in Palestine for the Jewish people.

By 1914, the pressure of political activity and academic work were beginning to weigh heavily upon him. Returning from Switzerland in August that year, he found a War Office circular on his desk. The document invited scientists who had made discoveries of possible military importance to submit them to the UK Government. Unknown to him at the time, the event was to mark a significant turning point in his career.

The biochemist had previously worked on a fermentation process and he made details of this available to the Government, generously asking for no remuneration.

Nothing was heard until spring 1916, when the biochemist received a visit from Dr. Rintoul, the chief research chemist of Nobel, a leading explosives manufacturer. Rintoul checked the biochemist's laboratory notebooks, which contained his experimental work. After this, arrangements were made for the director of Nobel's to come to Manchester with two of his chemists. The fermentation experiments were successfully repeated and a contract was offered and accepted. Alas, soon afterwards, the Nobel Scottish plant suffered a serious explosion and the company was released from its contractual obligations.

In March 1916, the biochemist's university career was interrupted once more when he was approached by Sir Frederick Nathan, the head of the Admiralty powder department. Nathan asked for help and explained that there was a serious

The Clock Mill at Three Mills, Bromley by Bow, London E3.

shortage of acetone, a solvent used in the making of cordite, a smokeless explosive made from gun cotton. The challenge was immediately taken up by the biochemist, who spent four days of his week in Manchester and the remaining three in London to set up a pilot plant to manufacture the solvent. The project was of such national importance that the biochemist was released from his university duties to concentrate on the war effort.

Later the biochemist was introduced to Winston Churchill, then the First Lord of the Admiralty, who explained: '... we need 30,000 tons of acetone', and asked: 'Can you make it?'

With powerful people like Churchill behind him, the biochemist was able to assemble a team and find new premises for his large-scale pioneering experiments. The plant chosen was the Nicholson gin distillery, housed in the Clock Mill at Bromley by Bow (the site currently known as Three Mills).

After many months of disappointment the process was at last regularly producing half a ton of material. When the Admiralty was satisfied with the results, arrangements were made to convert several distilleries in Britain to the new process. A programme was then rapidly instigated to train chemists to run these new production plants. Later, owing to wartime shortages of grain, a main ingredient in the acetone distillation process, a large part of the production was transferred to Canada and other countries where plentiful cereal supplies existed.

While these activities were going on, the biochemist, Dr. Chaim Weizmann, had become recognised as a prominent figure in the British Zionist cause, becoming leader of the World Zionist movement by 1920. Working for the Admiralty had brought Weizmann into contact with many powerful people including Arthur James Balfour who had replaced Sir Edward Grey as the UK Foreign Secretary. In November 1917, Balfour issued his famous Declaration giving Britain's support for the establishment of a Jewish national home in Palestine.

Dr. Chaim Weizmann (1874-1952), the first President of the State of Israel.

Weizmann was rewarded for his hard work and dedication in 1948 when he was elected the first President of the State of Israel. So it could be said that a little known site at the foot of the Lea Valley (Three Mills at Bromley by Bow) played an influential part in world history, first by helping the Allies secure peace in the Great War and secondly by promoting the career of this now famous man.

REFERENCES
Gardner, E.M., *The Three Mills—Bromley by Bow* (The River Lea Tidal Mill Trust, 1957)
Weizmann, Chaim, *Trial and Error: the Autobiography of Chaim Weizmann* (Hamish Hamilton, 1949)

The Women who Influenced the Lea Valley Industries

HERE, in the 20th century, it is not unusual for women to experience discrimination in the workplace when striving to gain equal status with their male counterparts. Think how much more difficult it would have been for women, in the 18th and 19th centuries, to have influenced decision-making or to have gained a position of authority within the industries in which they worked.

When William Walton, a producer of gunpowder at Balham in Surrey and Waltham Abbey in Essex, died intestate in 1711 his widow Philippa was effectively forced to take over the business. At the age of 35, with 10 children to care for, she could have been forgiven if she had taken the easy option of selling her late husband's company and enjoying the proceeds. Philippa, however, was made of sterner stuff. She ran the company on behalf of herself and her children for 12 years, only allowing her second eldest son John to purchase a 25 per cent share for £2,500 in January 1723.

The relatively peaceful period after 1714 saw the demand for gunpowder decline, forcing many producers out of business. Again Philippa demonstrated great determination and business acumen by concentrating manufacture at the Waltham Abbey plant, which meant closing down the operation at Balham. In this way she was able to improve the commercial viability of her company while still remaining one of the largest suppliers of gunpowder to the British Government.

A further example of the influence of women upon the Lea Valley industry, although in a different area, could also be seen at a much later time.

Towards the latter part of the 19th century, at the southern end of the Lea Valley, there developed what was to become one of the most famous industrial disputes in British history. The Fabian lecturer Annie Besant, in 1888, had written an article in her weekly newspaper *Link* drawing attention to the plight of the women working in the dangerous occupation of match-making. At the time, the principal employer was Bryant & May who had established a large factory in the east end of London at Bow.

Apart from the women having to endure long hours, low wages and fines for talking during the monotonous production operations, many had their lives dramatically shortened or suffered severe physical injury from working with the chemical phosphorous, a highly toxic substance. Workers who handled the material could find that the toxin had been absorbed into the body causing bone deterioration and teeth to fall out. It has also been reported that workers badly affected by the chemical would glow in the dark.

Besant's article provoked a strike amongst the 700 women matchmakers who walked out of work. The publicity created by the women's action brought strong public sympathy and support for their cause. Startled by the solidarity of the walk-out and the strength of public

A plaque erected in Saint Michael's Church, Mickleham, Surrey to the memory of Philippa Walton (1675-1749).

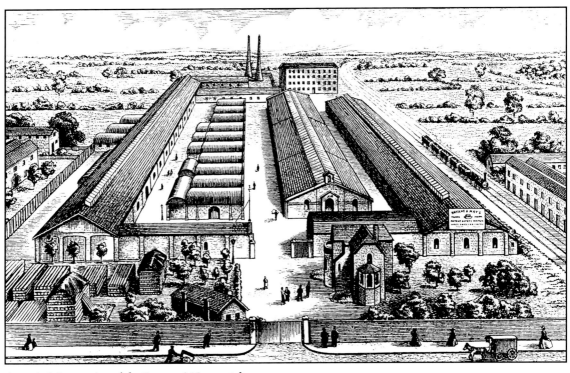

*An artist's impression of the Bryant & May match
factory at Bow, east London in 1861.*

*Annie Besant (1847-1933).
President of the
Theosophical Society,
author and lecturer.*

*Eleanor Marx (1855-1898),
youngest daughter of Karl.*

*Procession of match makers on their way to
Westminster 1888.*

Women posing for the photographer on the Bryant & May match factory production line at Bow, east London, c.1890.

support, the company finally conceded to almost every demand made by the strikers. At the time, given the low regard in which women factory workers were held, having in the main to do the most menial jobs, the walk-out was an extremely courageous act considering the vulnerability of this group of workers. While some have suggested that the strike was provoked by a comfortably-off middle-class campaigner, with nothing to lose, it does show that given the right circumstances, in this case the intolerable working conditions, woman-power was present in the 19th century.

In March 1889, considerably encouraged by what the neighbouring women matchmakers had achieved, Will Thorne, an illiterate labourer working at the Beckton Gas Works in East Ham, was able to recruit some 20,000 fellow workers to trade union membership. The task took Thorne only four months to complete and he was ably assisted in his endeavours by Eleanor Marx, the daughter of Karl. With the backing of an organised workforce behind him, Thorne could now negotiate from a position of strength. He was able to get the South Metropolitan Gas Company to change their method of working from a two-shift to a three-shift system. This was a landmark victory for the time, as it meant a cut in the basic working day from 12 to eight hours. Fearing industrial action, other gas companies soon followed the example set at Beckton and changed their conditions of work. Meanwhile, the ripples of victory emanating from the action of the women matchmakers extended further than Beckton.

Close to the district of Bow reside the London Docks. Here it was common practice to employ casual rather than permanent labour with workers being engaged on a daily basis. This, combined with poor wages, was a constant source of irritation amongst the workforce. In summer 1889, with the gains of the women matchmakers and the Beckton gas-workers still fresh in people's minds, the Port of London dockers struck for a wage increase from around four pence to six pence an hour. After several weeks of bitter struggle and with the support of other sympathetic trade unions, the 'dockers' tanner' was won.

As the 20th century draws to a close can we say that the role of modern industrial woman has progressed to one of total equality of career opportunity and workplace influence with that of her male counterpart?

REFERENCES
Fairclough, Keith, 'Philippa Walton, Gunpowder Producer at Waltham Abbey', *Essex Journal* (Spring 1996)
Pelling, Henry, *A History of British Trade Unionism* (Pelican Books, 1976)

Note: For a fuller account of Philippa Walton and the gunpowder widows, it is recommended that the reader consults the articles by Dr. Keith Fairclough (listed above) published in *Essex Journal*.

7 From Gunpowder to Tourism—the Peaceful Explosion

THE ROYAL GUNPOWDER MILLS at Waltham Abbey, which occupy some 190 acres towards the northern end of the Lea Valley, were in continuous Government use from 1787 to 1991. Before this, gunpowder had been produced on the site by the Walton family.

Until steam was introduced in the 1850s, water from the River Lea powered the machinery and charged the site's dual-level canal system. In the 20th century, the development and manufacture of a range of chemical propellants and explosives, particularly tetryl and RDX (used in the 'dam busters' raid) helped the Allied Forces to win two world wars. The site, now decommissioned, contains over 300 structures of which 21 are listed.

The experimental, development and production work carried out at Waltham Abbey has, over the centuries, provided employment and brought economic and social prosperity to the area. Neither was this work for entirely military purposes. The peaceful use of explosives in civil engineering has speeded the construction of roads, bridges, railways, canals and harbours and made the extraction of essential raw materials considerably easier in the mining and quarrying industries. Due to the quality of Waltham Abbey's products, which were recognised internationally, new export markets were opened up to Britain.

With the closure of the mills economic hardship came to the locality. The question then had to be addressed as to whether any commercial alternatives could be put in place. Solutions to such problems often depend upon a site's particular heritage and accessibility to transport. If a stricken industry or place of manufacture has an interesting historic past, then there is the possibility of developing a long-term strategy based on aspects of heritage.

Waltham Abbey for many reasons is truly the jewel in the tourism and heritage crown, the site being recognised by English Heritage as '...the most important to the history of explosives manufacture in Europe'. The Royal Commission on the Historical Monuments of England (RCHME) have said that the Gunpowder Mills are '... the most complex industrial site yet surveyed by the commission'. There are also at least thirty-eight A4 pages of references to individual historical documents on the Waltham Abbey Mills located at the Public Record Office, Kew. As those who seriously study history will know, such a wealth of quality documented evidence is extremely rare.

Powder barges on the dual level canal system at the Royal Gunpowder Mills at Waltham Abbey. These barges were used for transporting explosive material around the site and not for shipping gunpowder, via the River Lea, to the powder magazines located along the River Thames and elsewhere.

Men and women process workers at the Royal Gunpowder Mills, Waltham Abbey, c.1910.

Because the site had remained in Government hands for so long (over two hundred years) and because of the highly secret nature of the work, the place took on the mantle of a forbidden city. External contractors for repair and maintenance were seldom used, the work being carried out internally by a highly skilled workforce who had to comply with the rigours of the Official Secrets Act. These were major factors in the conservation of the site which have clearly helped to guard the integrity of the artefacts.

When a particular source of power for the site's machinery became obsolete, or outlived its useful life, it was replaced with the latest technology. The abandoned technology was then discarded and allowed to fall slowly into decay. This has provided a unique opportunity to trace,

Remains of mid-19th-century water powered gunpowder press house on the site of the Royal Gunpowder Mills, Waltham Abbey, Essex.

study and record the technological changes to the energy sources which drove the various pieces of processing plant, from water through steam to electricity. Apart from the obvious educational and academic benefits to be derived from such work, much can be learned from studying the past and making comparisons with evolving present-day industrial and technological developments. By a careful analysis of the results, it is often possible to learn important lessons and avoid repeating costly mistakes.

Listed incorporating mills at the Royal Gunpowder Mills, Waltham Abbey, Essex. Picture taken in autumn 1996.

The northern end of the Gunpowder Mills site has been designated a Site of Special Scientific Interest (SSSI) by English Nature. Planted in the 17th century with alder trees to provide charcoal for the production of gunpowder, the wood now supports the largest heronry in Essex and one of the biggest flocks of siskin (a small yellow-green bird, not unlike the greenfinch) in the UK. In seclusion, and protected by the dense vegetation, live a variety of mammals such as deer, foxes and otters. Here by man's deliberate interference with nature, we have been accidentally provided with a priceless environmental asset over two hundred years later.

After an extensive programme of decontamination—with the cost of £16 million being met by the Ministry of Defence—a Charitable Trust has been formed to own, conserve and manage the Gunpowder Mills for the benefit of the public. A further role for the Trust is to formulate a strategy for the creation of a large visitor attraction. The site's heritage will be exploited through the promotion of a plan which will interpret the various processes used in the manufacture of gunpowder. This initiative is well under way, boosted by a grant (in 1997) of £6.5 million from the Heritage Lottery Fund.

While the change of emphasis from manufacturing to tourism will not necessarily bring instant economic benefit to the region, there is the hope that in the longer term the sensitive restoration of many treasured sites within the Lea Valley will create a focus of attention which will encourage new job-creating industries back to the area. After all, we have the model of Ironbridge Gorge and Coalbrookdale, where the unique industrial heritage of the region helped secure considerable manufacturing investment, particularly from abroad, in the nearby town of Telford.

REFERENCES

Bone, Daniel, 'The Royal Gunpowder Mills' publicity brochure (Civix, September 1992)

Lewis, Jim, 'The Lea Valley and Britain's Forgotten Greatness', *Electrotechnology* (December 1997/ January 1998)

A Bright Light Comes to Ponders End and the World is Changed

IN 1886, Joseph Wilson Swan (1828-1914) (later Sir) moved his lamp factory from South Benwell in north-east England to a site beside the River Lea at Ponders End, Enfield. Although Swan had demonstrated a crude form of electric lamp almost twenty years before the American Thomas Alva Edison had registered his own version, he had failed to patent the device. Swan had naively believed that the technology he had used was already in the public domain and well understood. Rather than fight an expensive legal battle in the courts over the invention, Swan joined with Edison and the Ediswan Company (as it eventually became known) was formed.

John Ambrose Fleming (1849-1945), a prominent scientist, was invited to join the company as a consultant to investigate the blackening on the inside of light bulbs, resulting from the 'Edison effect'. This had been primarily caused, in Swan's case, by carbon deposits released from his unique cellulosed thread filaments. Fleming had the Ponders End laboratory make a number of lamps with an extra electrode (anode) on which he carried out his experiments.

Sir Joseph Wilson Swan, F.R.S. (1828-1914)

After completing his work, Fleming took an extra consultancy with the Marconi Wireless Telegraph Company. Being involved with Marconi may have given him the idea of improving the method for the detection of radio waves. Until then, the favoured device for detection was the coherer, an insulated tube filled with loose iron particles which conducted when a signal was applied. The device had the distinct disadvantage of having to be gently tapped after each operation to free the particles ready for the next signal.

In 1904, Fleming registered an improved version of his earlier experimental device, the world's first thermionic valve, a diode, (two electrode) British Patent No.24850. The term 'valve' was borrowed from mechanical nomenclature and implies a means of control. In the electronic sense, the diode valve controls the passage of an oscillating radio wave by allowing it to pass in only one direction. This is the method of detection which, after suitable processing, allows our radio receivers to convert the radio signals which have been transmitted from the numerous broadcast stations around the world into intelligible speech and music.

Professor Ambrose Fleming (1849-1945).

It was perhaps fitting that the patenting of Fleming's device had, in a way, made up for Edison claiming the invention of the electric lamp ahead of Swan. Edison himself, in the early 1880s, had concluded that the blackening on the inside of the light bulb was caused by electrically charged particles of carbon flowing as a current stream from the filament. He had also concluded that the current in the bulb varied with the temperature of the filament. This, he observed, was directly related to the supply voltage. Apart from constructing an 'electrical indicator' as a result of his experiments, it would appear that Edison had not attached any other commercial value to his discovery.

However, it was Fleming's understanding, and his commercial grasp, of the importance of Edison's discoveries regarding the electron emissions as current flow from a heated filament which allowed him to seize a missed opportunity which he exploited. Appreciating what Edison had missed, and also understanding the

Swan's first practical incandescent lamp (sample made in 1877).

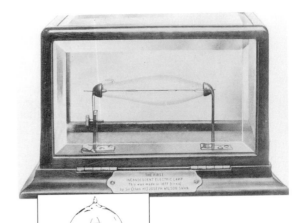

requirements for the detection of an oscillating wave, Fleming was uniquely positioned to make the discovery of the century. With the modified light bulbs from Ponders End, Fleming was able to bring together, for the first time, the technology of the lamp and the electronic control of a wireless signal. With the extra electrode (anode) the electric lamp had effectively become the diode valve.

In a way, Fleming's discovery might be considered an act of fate, or perhaps natural justice, as he had made up for Swan's slowness in registering his invention before the American.

It can be claimed, on the basis of Fleming's work on Swan's electric lamp, that the post-industrial revolution—the technological revolution—began at Ponders End, Enfield. The diode valve was only one of many exciting industrial firsts for the Lea Valley region. From this simple beginning has grown the multimedia

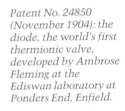

Patent No. 24850 (November 1904): the diode, the world's first thermionic valve, developed by Ambrose Fleming at the Ediswan laboratory at Ponders End, Enfield.

Ediswan lamp factory at Ponders End, Enfield c.1903.

The last remaining utilised building, constructed 1890, from the Ediswan Works at Ponders End, Enfield. Currently (1998) the building is occupied by one of the Amstrad group of companies.

communications industry of today and the way has been paved for even more exciting technological developments in industry, entertainment and leisure.

At the present rate of electronic progress it is almost impossible to imagine the state of communications technology 86 years hence (the lifetime of Swan) who had himself pioneered and witnessed many remarkable scientific achievements which, for the day, would have probably seemed equally unimaginable.

REFERENCES

Author unknown, *The Pageant of the Lamp* (The Edison Swan Electric Company Ltd.)

Birchall, Derek, 'On the Relative Importance of Relevance and Irrelevance', John D. Rose Memorial Lecture, London, 2 June 1982, *Chemistry and Industry* (18 July 1983)

Karwatka, Dennis, *Technology's Past* (Prakken Publications Inc., Kentucky, 1996)

Lewis, Jim, 'The Lea Valley and Britain's Forgotten Greatness', *Electrotechnology* (December 1997/ January 1998)

Munt, Brian, 'A Short History of Ediswan', unpublished paper (Dover, 1989)

Shiers, George, 'The First Electron Tube', *Scientific American*, vol.220, no.3 (March 1969)

Note: Apart from the diode valve being a 'spin-off' from Swan's early work on the incandescent lamp, two other world 'firsts' emanated from his experimentation. The discovery of the first commercial man-made fibre, known as 'Artificial Silk', came from Swan's search for a suitable material for his lamp filaments. Courtauld, a major chemical manufacturer which eventually became part of the giant Imperial Chemical Industries (ICI), continued the development which resulted in the fabric 'Courtelle'.

The techniques which were developed at Ponders End to evacuate the glass light bulbs of air attracted the attention of Sir James Dewar who arranged to have his prototype vacuum flasks made there (see chapter 'Creating a Vacuum at Ponders End').

Electrical Connections in the Lea Valley

WHAT'S IN A NAME? It is certainly the comfort factor when buying a piece of electrical equipment, as we are soothingly reassured by the familiar brand that our purchase can be trusted. Over the decades the Lea Valley has produced a catalogue of household favourites particularly within the electrical and electronic industries—Belling, Belling & Lee, Ediswan, MK and Thorn to name but a few. It is interesting to note the connections between the founding entrepreneurs of these famous companies. Unconsciously, these people brought together a grouping of electrical and electronic industries within the Lea Valley which made the region unique. Although this has generally gone unnoticed, it is probably fair to say that there are few places of similar geographic size, anywhere in the world, which are able to claim the design, development and production of so many innovative products and projects over a period of more than one hundred years.

Below. Charles Arnold (third from left in front row) with original Park Road employees in 1952.

Charles Reginald Belling

Around the turn of the century at Chelmsford, Essex, two young men served their apprenticeship together at the Crompton Electrical Company. Their names were Charles Leonard Arnold and Charles Reginald Belling. In 1912 they were to form, with H.E. How, Belling & Company, which was to revolutionise the manufacture of the electric fire element by constructing it upon a piece of fireclay. This device received a British patent in 1912, a world

Women working in the MK metal pressing shop, c.1960.

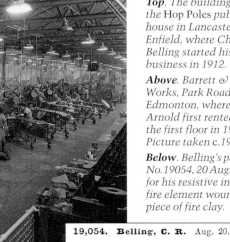

Top. The building, behind the Hop Poles *public house in Lancaster Road, Enfield, where Charles Belling started his business in 1912.*

Above. Barrett & Sons *Works, Park Road, Edmonton, where Charles Arnold first rented part of the first floor in 1919. Picture taken c.1951.*

Below. Belling's patent *No.19054, 20 August 1912, for his resistive infra-red fire element wound on a piece of fire clay.*

19,054. Belling, C. R. Aug. 20.

FIG.1. FIG.3.

Heating by electricity.—A heater, shown in elevation and cross-section in Figs. 1 and 3, respectively, comprises a wire *d* wound on one

first. Before, the element had been encased in a quartz tube. This simple invention is still heating our homes and cooking our food as the millennium approaches and will conceivably carry on doing so for some time beyond.

R.E. Crompton, who had founded his company in 1878, had in 1881 acted as Chief Engineer to the Swan United Electric Light Company Limited. Joseph Swan (later Sir), who should have claimed the invention of the electric lamp for Britain, failed to do so. He naively believed the technology he had used was in the public domain. It was his American counterpart, Thomas Alva Edison, who patented his device first. Fortunately common sense prevailed and the two men formed a joint company which was eventually to become 'Ediswan', located at Ponders End, Enfield.

From 1907, after his apprenticeship at Crompton's, Charles Belling worked as a superintendent of three departments at Ediswan's Ponders End factory until he joined again with Charles Arnold to form Belling & Co.

After a period of service in the Royal Artillery during the First World War, Arnold rejoined his old partner in 1919. Electrical energy for lighting, cooking and heating was a rapidly expanding market, although the technical improvements of plugs and sockets had not kept pace. The partners agreed that this problem should be addressed and a revolutionary domestic electrical connection system was born. Their new socket was named 'Multy Kontact'. Arnold now formed The Heavy Current Electrical Accessory Company with Belling as the 'sleeping partner'. After a shaky start, the company blossomed and in 1923 moved to a new purpose-built factory in Wakefield Street, Edmonton. Here the more familiar name of MK (from 'Multy Kontact') was adopted.

No doubt prompted by the first advertised radio broadcast (wireless as it was then known) in Britain, in June 1920, when Dame Nellie Melba gave a song recital from the Marconi Works in Chelmsford, Essex, and the commencement, two years later, of public service broadcasts from the famous 2LO Station at Savoy Hill, London, the electrical engineer Edgar Morton Lee approached Charles Belling for help. The

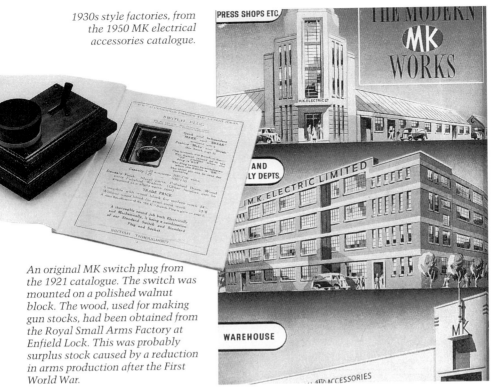

1930s style factories, from the 1950 MK electrical accessories catalogue.

An original MK switch plug from the 1921 catalogue. The switch was mounted on a polished walnut block. The wood, used for making gun stocks, had been obtained from the Royal Small Arms Factory at Enfield Lock. This was probably surplus stock caused by a reduction in arms production after the First World War.

Further expansion of Thorn's business took place when, in 1963, Ediswan Industrial CRTs (cathode ray tubes) was incorporated into the growing industrial grouping. The move demonstrates the almost uncanny bonding, over a considerable period of time, of the Lea Valley's electrical industries and their entrepreneurs, which further strengthened the 'electrical connections'.

Sadly, by the early 1980s, the Lea Valley's 'electrical connections' had started to become strained as the companies within this sector either changed hands or went out of business. The reasons for the demise of the electrical and electronic sector of the Lea Valley have never been fully explained or analysed in detail. It might be argued that the increasing pressure from cheap imports of electrical and electronic goods, particularly from the Far East, had been a major contributory factor for the failure of the Lea Valley industry. However, this does not fully explain why a once prosperous regional industry, which had taken over one hundred years to advance and which had produced a number of innovative world firsts should disappear, almost without trace, within a decade.

partnership of Belling & Lee Limited was formed in 1922 when it was decided to manufacture mains operated valve wireless receivers in a small factory in Queensway, Ponders End. Not surprisingly the valves were supplied by the Ediswan Company, further strengthening the Lea Valley 'electrical connections'.

When, in 1936, the British Broadcasting Corporation (BBC) began the world's first high definition public television service transmissions from the studios at Alexandra Palace, Wood Green, on the western slopes of the Lea Valley, the valves for the transmitters were supplied by the Ediswan Company.

By 1961, after negotiations between Thorn Electrical Industries (TEI) and the General Electric Company (GEC), Thorn AEI Radio Valves & Tubes Limited was formed. This increased the size of Jules Thorn's (later Sir) already considerable industrial empire. Interestingly, Arnold Weinstock (later Lord), the owner and chief executive of GEC, was born at Stoke Newington, in the London borough of Hackney, situated in the Lea Valley.

REFERENCES

Munt, Brian E., *A Short History of Ediswan, Mazda and Brima* (Dover, 1989)

The Pageant of the Lamp (The Edison Swan Electric Company Ltd.)

Pandit, S.A., *From Making to Music—The History of Thorn EMI* (Hodder & Stoughton, 1996)

O Creating a Vacuum at Ponders End

JAMES DEWAR (later Sir James), was born at Kincardine-on-Forth, Scotland, on 20 September 1842. At the time it would have been impossible to have guessed that the professional path he was eventually to tread would lead him to the Lea Valley.

Dewar's early school years were hindered by rheumatic fever which laid him low at the age of ten. The attack was said to have been caused by Dewar falling through the ice when playing near his home. On regaining his health he was sent to a private academy and afterwards, in 1858, he went on to Edinburgh University. There he worked under James David Forbes, Professor of Natural Philosophy and later under Lord Lyon Playfair, Professor of Chemistry, whose demonstrator he became. When Playfair resigned his post, Dewar became demonstrator to his successor, Alexander Crum Brown.

In 1869 Dewar was appointed lecturer on chemistry and later received a Professorship with the Royal Veterinary College. Dewar left Scotland for Cambridge in 1875 after being elected to the Jacksonian Chair of Natural Experimental Philosophy. Within two years he was elected Fullerian Professor of Chemistry at the Royal Institute of Great Britain, London. Dewar held both these chairs until his death on 27 March 1923.

There is no doubt, as evidenced by the large amount of published material, that Dewar was an avid and skilful experimenter. In a paper published in the *Transactions of the Royal Society*, Edinburgh, 1873, 'On the Physical Constants of Hydrogenium', Dewar illustrated his experiment with a diagram showing a twin walled '… stout brass envelope, thoroughly exhausted of air …'. This is probably one of the earliest references to what we would recognise today as a vacuum flask.

Perhaps by a fortunate twist of fate, Dewar, with several other eminent scientists of the day, was called to the Ediswan electric lamp factory at Ponders End, Enfield in 1888. At the time the company was involved in a major court case

Sir James Dewar (1842-1923).

which concerned infringements of their patent by other lamp manufacturers. The scientists were engaged to carry out experiments relating to the alleged infringements and also to act as expert witnesses on behalf of the Ediswan company. Another of the team was Professor Ambrose Fleming (later Sir Ambrose), a respected scientist. It would appear that he and Dewar formed a close working relationship, as evidenced by the considerable number of scientific papers they published jointly between 1893 and 1898.

By the early 1870s, after much experimentation, Dewar had perfected a method to produce liquid oxygen in quantity. However, the liquid, at its normal temperature of minus 182 degrees Celsius, was inclined to boil away rapidly if kept in an open vessel. When discussing experiments involving liquid oxygen with Ambrose Fleming, perhaps at the time when they were working at the Ediswan lamp factory, it has been recorded that Dewar handed Fleming a sketch of a double-walled glass vessel.

Fleming, at the time, was carrying out experiments on electric lamps which

incorporated both glass and vacuum technology and he was no doubt seen by Dewar as the person most experienced in producing a vessel with the air evacuated from between the double-walls. This was successfully done at the Ponders End factory and the more familiar type of vacuum flask, or 'Dewar Vessel' as it was originally named, was born.

The improved thermal insulation of the flask not only provided Dewar with the opportunity to enhance his demonstrations before the Royal Society, but it also helped him considerably with his experiments into liquefying different gases. After several years of painstaking experiments, Dewar successfully succeeded in 'silvering' the inner walls of the vacuum flask by introducing a small quantity of mercury as a gas. This improved the efficiency of the flask by providing a reflective coating which reduced losses from radiated heat. However, it is doubtful at this stage in the flask's development if Dewar appreciated the considerable commercial potential which lay ahead for others to exploit.

In fact the commercial future for the vacuum flask was not that far away. By 1907 a group of British businessmen, led by Milton Bartholomew, acquired the patent rights to manufacture the now familiarly named 'Thermos flask' in the British Empire, South America and other selected

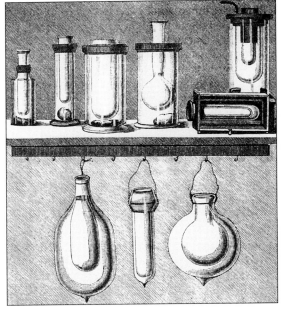

Early specimens of containers for holding liquid gas. In the top row can be seen containers with the chemical phosphoric anhydride between walls (shown as a piece of material) to absorb moisture. The bottom row shows early vacuum vessels. In early experiments with liquid gasses, scientists wished to observe the liquid by viewing its behaviour through the walls of the container. Vacuum vessels, because of their glass construction, were ideal for such experiments.

parts of the world. The brand name 'Thermos' (derived from the Greek word 'therme' meaning heat) had originated in Germany some three years earlier where development of the vacuum flask towards a commercial product had been carried out by Reinhold Burger, a partner in the firm of Burger and Aschenbrenner, Berlin. Burger was a former pupil of Dewar and had gone into partnership on return to his native Germany with what would appear to have been the specific purpose of developing a commercially viable vacuum product.

The first Thermos manufacturing facility in Britain opened in Tottenham, north London in 1908 in an 8,000-square feet factory. Production

Thermos Flask advertisement 1909.

was relatively slow as each glass flask (known in the trade as a filler) had to be individually blown by skilled tradesmen who were only able to produce around ten units per day. By 1911, Thermos had installed new machinery to manufacture and increase the production rate of the glass filler. This had the effect of reducing the cost of a typical half-pint flask by over eighty per cent, making the product available to a wider customer base.

When the First World War commenced in 1914 the factory, in keeping with many others, was taken over by the Ministry of Munitions to manufacture shell cases for the armed forces. Unfortunately the factory was destroyed by fire in 1917 after being bombed by a Zeppelin airship. However, by 1918 a new and larger factory had been opened in Fontayne Road, Tottenham, not only to replace the one which had been destroyed but to help cope with future demand. Restructuring of the company took place in the early 1920s when the Thermos Bottle Company of America took a controlling interest in the British manufacturer. After reorganisation the company became Thermos (1925) Limited.

Further expansion within the Lea Valley took place when a new glass filler factory opened in Hackney in 1931 followed by a metal canister factory in Leyton. By 1938, Tottenham production was moved to Leyton as the company's expansion continued. When the Second World War commenced in 1939, the Thermos flask had become so much a part of every-day life that the factories were left to continue production of flasks for the armed services and civilians. In fact the flask was so popular with the Air Force that it was the proud boast of Thermos that 'every time a thousand allied bombers went on a raid, there were anything from 10,000 to 12,000 THERMOS brand vacuum flasks in the air as well'.

REFERENCES

Author unknown, *The Pageant of the Lamp* (The Edison Swan Electric Company Ltd.)

Author unknown, 'Vacuum Flask History', *The Ironmonger* (16 February 1957)

Author unknown, *The History and Technology of the Vacuum Flask* (Thermos Limited, Brentwood, 1989)

Dewar, Lady (ed.), *Collected Papers of Sir James Dewar*, vol.2 (Cambridge University Press, 1927)

Weaver, J.R.H. (ed.), *Dictionary of National Biography 1922-1930* (Oxford University Press)

The Lea Valley—Birthplace of Television Broadcasting

ON SATURDAY 2 November 1936, at precisely 3p.m., the world's first public service (high definition) television broadcasts began from a relatively unknown site, in international terms, in North London. Transmissions commenced on that momentous day from the studios of the British Broadcasting Corporation (BBC) located at Alexandra Palace, Wood Green. The transmitter mast, now a famous landmark, is positioned at the south-eastern end of the building and can be seen silhouetted on the ridge of the western slopes of the Lea Valley. It no longer broadcasts television pictures.

In the beginning only a small number of affluent Londoners could receive the limited monochrome (black and white) television broadcasts, but the medium's popularity rapidly grew and has since been adopted throughout the world as one of the main forms of entertainment. Now that colour television has become the norm, with services drawing on material from international providers through cable and satellite communication, it is almost impossible for anyone not to have had their lives influenced, one way or another, by this addictive medium. With today's rapid advances in technology, such as interactive television and digitally coded transmissions, it may be difficult for young people to imagine the extreme limitations of the embryonic public service broadcasts.

John Logie Baird, a Scotsman, has been credited by many people as the inventor of television but this is not strictly true. Like most discoveries and inventions, there is nearly always previous or parallel work by other individuals. This was certainly true in the case of television, although Baird must be given credit for his tenacity and perseverance, living in abject poverty while trying to perfect his system. However, on the other side of the Atlantic, at about the same time that Baird was carrying out his experiments, another inventive genius was working on an electronic method of transmitting picture information.

Vladimir Kosma Zworykin, a Russian emigré, was involved in the development of radio valves and photo-electric cells for the Westinghouse Electric and Manufacturing Company in Pittsburg. In 1923 he applied for a U.S. patent for his invention, the iconoscope. This device was essentially an early electronic camera tube. The following year he demonstrated a crude television system, only to be politely told by his employers that '… it might be better if [he] spent [his] time on something more useful'.

Baird's first public demonstration of television, in April 1925, was at the department store of Selfridge in London. The system he had developed to receive his pictures was electro-mechanical using a 30-hole Nipkow disc driven by an electric motor. The revolving disc scanned a modulated electric lamp which obtained its signals from the output stage of a standard domestic wireless, the picture information being transmitted in the normal radio spectrum. Baird's method of picture transmission was also electro-

Above. *Engraving showing general view of Alexandra Palace and Park c.1875.*

mechanical, whereas Zworykin had experimented with a system which was completely electronic.

An all electronic high definition television system had also been developed by Electrical Musical Industries (EMI), under Isaac Shoenberg during the early 1930s. The EMI system used a cathode ray tube to view the picture and an electronic camera tube (Emitron) to scan the scene to be transmitted. It is probable that the EMI team had been able to 'borrow' from Zworykin's work on the iconoscope.

Two separate studios, which remain today, were set up at Alexandra Palace to allow the BBC to evaluate both television systems. As may be imagined, it was the electronic system (405 line) which was eventually chosen.

Alexandra Palace was first opened in 1873. The inspiration to create a centre for the recreation and enjoyment of the populace, 'The People's Palace', came after the Great Exhibition of 1851, situated in the Crystal Palace which was temporarily erected in London's Hyde Park. 'Ally Pally', as it affectionately became known, suffered a tragic fire 16 days after opening and

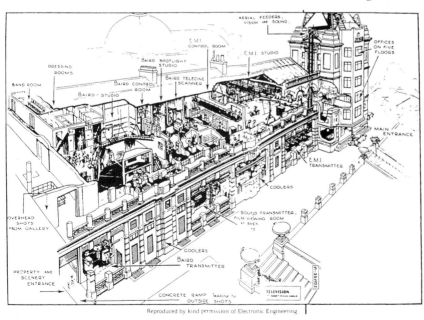

Reproduced by kind permission of Electronic Engineering

Diagram showing the layout of the early Baird and EMI studios at Alexandra Palace, Wood Green, c.1936.

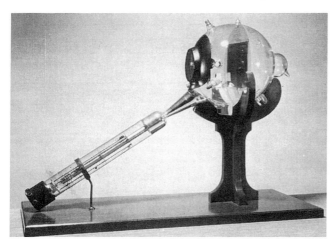

The 'Emitron' camera tube worked on the same principle as Zworkin's 'Iconoscope'. These two devices were developed independently. On the 'Emitron' the optical image was formed on the same side of the 'target' as was scanned by the electron beam, the electron gun being offset, and it was this feature which imposed the characteristic shape on the TV camera.

Above. A scene from Journeys End. R.C. Sherriff's play, transmitted 19 March 1954, was the last to be produced at Alexandra Palace.

Left. BBC 'Emitron' TV camera, c.1937. Note the characteristic 'droop-snoot' shape.

was destroyed. In the short period before its loss the Palace had rapidly become a popular place of entertainment, attracting over 124,000 visitors. Less than two years after its destruction, the new Palace opened its doors to the public in May 1875, bestowing art and culture upon its Victorian visitors.

One hundred and five years after re-opening tragedy struck again when the Palace suffered its second fire in July 1980. The Great Hall and surrounding area suffered considerable damage. Fortunately the Palm Court and the two historic BBC studios, which had stood empty for some years, escaped the tragedy.

After many years of funding problems and neglect, 'The Peoples' Palace' looks set once more for a new lease of life. In recent times the Alexandra Palace and Park Board of Trustees, a charitable trust responsible for running the

Models at the Radiolympia exhibition in 1947 viewing a picture in the mirror (the cathode ray tube being mounted vertically) on what appears to be an E K Cole (Ekco) television receiver.

Palace and Park, announced that the Treasury Solicitor will allow the Trust to proceed with the proposed development of the Palace. The second piece of good news came on 1 October 1996, when the Department of National Heritage conferred Grade II listed status upon it. It is hoped that this news will once more herald the rising of 'The People's Palace', now a world landmark in communication heritage, to the status of its Victorian heyday. This would no doubt be welcomed enthusiastically by the national and international television community and give pride and pleasure to people locally.

REFERENCES

Author unknown, *Alexandra Palace, 'A Substantial Development Opportunity'* (London Borough of Haringey, 1996)

Bridgewater, T.H., 'Just a Few Lines', Supplement to the *Bulletin of the British Vintage Wireless Society*, Robert Hawes (ed.) (BVWS, August 1992)

Geddes, Keith, *The Setmakers, a History of the Radio and Television Industry* (The British Radio & Electronic Equipment Manufacturer's Association, 1991)

Karwatka, Dennis, *Technology's Past* (Prakken Publications Inc., Kentucky, 1996)

Note: The Nipkow disc was named after its German inventor, Paul Nipkow, who patented the device in 1884. Baird used a 20-inch version of the disc, made of aluminium with 30 holes arranged in a spiral close to its outer edge, driven by an electric motor. At the TV receiver the disc was made to rotate (scan) in front of a neon lamp, each revolution producing a series of 30 vertical arcs. The filament of the lamp was arranged to alter in brightness which corresponded to the transmitted television signal. By 'scanning' the lamp as described 12½ times every second, using this mechanical method, a crude flickering picture could be built up.

At the TV transmitter, the light from the scene to be sent was focused through a lens and passed through the respective holes in the Nipkow disc. Located behind the disc was a photo-electric cell (instead of the lamp in the receiver) which converted the varying light energy from the scene into a corresponding series of electrical signals. The electro-mechanical system, compared with the electronic system, was very inefficient as only a small amount of light could pass through the disc.

VISITORS TO LONDON are reminded of Britain's past by statues and monuments erected to celebrate kings, queens, admirals and generals. To a much lesser degree do we see civic recognition given to the industrialists, manufacturers, engineers and entrepreneurs who not only made a significant contribution to the economic wealth of Britain but also shaped the way we live today.

One such industrialist, who received many glowing tributes in his lifetime, has been partially forgotten. This man, although small in stature, remains for the author, and for many others who worked for him, a giant in the world of electrical and electronic design and production. The late Sir Jules Thorn's international manufacturing empire, in its heyday, provided work for over 80,000 people. A large part of his workforce were resident in the Lea Valley.

Jules Thorn was born in Vienna in February 1899 and first came to Britain in 1923 as the sales representative of an Austrian gas mantle manufacturer. By the 1920s the days of gas lighting were numbered because of the increasing popularity and greater efficiency of electricity and the manufacturer went into liquidation in 1926. It is probably fair to assume, however, that Thorn's early involvement with lighting products had allowed him to sense a unique business opportunity.

At the time in Britain, the majority market for electric lamps was controlled by the Electric Lamp Manufacturers Association (ELMA). In those days, before the setting up of the Monopolies Commission, ELMA members strictly controlled the market price of the product.

In a courageously entrepreneurial spirit Thorn began importing lamps from Hungary and in 1928 he set up the Electric Lamp Service Company Limited which also dealt in radio components. This move no doubt would have been viewed with concern by ELMA who would have perceived the entry into the market of the 29-year-old Thorn as a threat to their profit margins. By the 1930s, with economic depression increasing, the Government placed severe tariffs on imported goods to protect the British manufacturing industry. While this action might have discouraged other men, not so Thorn. In fact it spurred him into seeking his own lamp manufacturing plant. In 1932 he acquired a relatively small lamp producer, the Atlas Lamp Works in Angel Road, Edmonton, which was not a member of ELMA. The previous year, in 1931, Thorn seems to have been gifted with extraordinary foresight, when he opened his first rental shop in Twickenham, Middlesex, hiring domestic radio receivers to the public.

In 1936, after buying the Ferguson Radio Corporation Limited, a company founded by J.B. Ferguson, a Canadian, Thorn set up a new factory in Lincoln Road, Enfield on the site of a former nursery. Ferguson had come to Britain in 1933 and began manufacturing radio receivers in a factory at Chiswick from imported component kits. However, he seems to have got into financial difficulties and there was the added problem that he only had a short lease on the premises.

After acquiring the company Thorn moved production to Enfield and J.B. Ferguson was engaged as general manager. He returned to Canada at the start of the Second World War and Thorn Electrical Industries, as it had been named after its flotation on the London Stock Market in 1936, retained the name of Ferguson which was to adorn many famous models of radio and television receivers.

After the cessation of hostilities, and with the resumption of television broadcasts by the BBC from its studios in Alexandra Palace, Wood Green in 1946, Ferguson began the design and production of its first television receivers. As Britain got back on its feet, public demand for television receivers grew. To meet this new challenge, Ferguson, by the mid-1950s, had to move its production facilities from Lincoln Road to a much larger factory complex at the junction of Southbury Road and the Great Cambridge Road, Enfield, only a few hundred metres away.

Sir Jules Thorn (1899-1980), founder of Thorn Electrical Industries.

The Ferguson stand at the 1952 Radio Show, Earl's Court, London. Note the way the televisions have been covered to stop the external light degrading the picture. Showing on the TV screens is the BBC test card 'C'.

In a relatively short period Jules Thorn, with a small team of talented executives, assembled a vast industrial empire mainly by acquiring established companies which in general supported other core activities within the group. In adopting such a policy, Thorn was frequently accused of having little interest in innovation and it was often suggested that he borrowed technology developed by others. While it is true that in many aspects of product manufacture Thorn was a follower of tried and tested technology, there were several occasions when his engineers led the world with innovative designs.

In 1967 colour television broadcasts began on BBC2, providing only a limited service of a few hours each week on 625 line, UHF. At the time, it should be remembered, the pre-war 405 line, VHF system was still providing the major part of television entertainment in monochrome (black and white). Therefore, to design, develop and manufacture new colour television receivers to service such meagre beginnings was a high-risk strategy for any company. Thorn met this challenge by encouraging his engineers to design and develop a completely new dual standard (405/625, VHF/UHF, monochrome/colour) large screen television receiver, the 2,000 series.

The 2,000 series was a mould-breaking world first, employing solid-state (all transistor) circuitry and a modular design. At the time, other colour television receivers used valve technology or were hybrids, a mixture of valves and semi-conductors. Thorn was well aware of the financial risks he was taking by allowing his engineers to proceed down an uncharted path, particularly as the electronic component industry had to be persuaded to support the project, they themselves having to develop new technologies and techniques.

To help speed development, a junior Ferguson engineer was despatched to the local Woolworth's store with instructions to buy the entire stock of plastic butter dishes. Back at the laboratory, these were converted, with a liberal helping of silicon rubber,

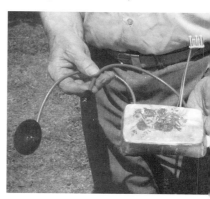

The hands of Sid Jones, Chief Ferguson Development Engineer, holding the original 2000 series prototype 'butter-dish' EHT multiplier.

Sid Westwood, Chief Engineer, Ferguson Advance Study Group, explaining the intricacies of satellite communication to Sir Richard Cave, Chairman of Thorn EMI (1981). In the background can be seen the former Ferguson laboratories and engineering centre—a supermarket now stands on this site in Enfield.

capacitors and stick rectifiers, into EHT (extra high tension) multipliers for an early batch trial. The point of these devices is to provide the final anode voltage, of about 25,000 volts for the cathode ray tube (CRT), without which no picture would be present on the viewing screen. Prior to this the method used for generating the EHT was through circuits employing thermionic valves. This technology had several drawbacks. One of these was the creation of dangerous radiation levels within the receiver which had to be carefully and expensively screened. The solid state EHT system employed by Thorn engineers did not suffer from such problems.

The 2,000 was quickly followed by the 3,000 series which was a single standard (625 line, UHF) solid-state model, the first commercial receiver to use a switched-mode power supply (chopper), the basis for present-day colour

television design. The speed of the 3,000 introduction so soon after the 2,000 series was influenced mainly by two factors—firstly, the increasing amount of colour material on 625 lines being put out by the broadcasters and, secondly, by the high cost of producing the dual standard 2,000 series. Sir Jules Thorn (he had been knighted in 1964), having supported the development of the original revolutionary solid-state design, had required his engineers to develop a cost effective sequel. He had remarked that he was 'having to put five pound notes into the back of each 2,000 series produced'.

It would be impossible in such a limited space to list all the world firsts in technological achievement, processes and products by the Thorn group of companies. However, there are a further two which are relevant to the Lea Valley. Working towards products which conserve our natural resources, Thorn Lighting Enfield launched two world firsts in the early 1980s. These were the 2D lamp and the Halogen cooker—cooking by light.

Sir Jules Thorn died on 12 December 1980 at the age of eighty-one. The industrial empire which he had created has now mostly been broken-up by those who came later to run his company in the 'modern style'; he had preferred a 'hands-on' approach.

On 9 December 1997, around eighty former Thorn employees gathered in the foyer of the Enfield Safeway superstore, which now stands on the site of the former Thorn EMI Ferguson engineering laboratories and manufacturing facilities, to witness the unveiling of a plaque to commemorate the contribution made to the world of technology by Sir Jules Thorn.

REFERENCES

Lewis, Jim, 'The Lea Valley and Britain's Forgotten Greatness', *Electrotechnology* (December 1997/January 1998)

Pandit, S.A., *From Making to Music* (Hodder & Stoughton, 1996)

Phillips, Cyril, 'Working for Sir Jules', *Electrical Times* (6 February 1981)

America Comes to Southgate

WHEN J. TAYLOR & SONS LTD., a manufacturer of vehicle engines, went into receivership in 1921, the 27-acre site in New Southgate, north London, adjacent to the Great Northern Railway, was bought by the American company, Western Electric. By the property standards of the day it would seem that Western Electric had got themselves a bargain, for it is recorded that the purchase price, in 1922, of the land and a two-storey building amounted to £80,000.

By the time of the Great War Western Electric had grown to be one of the largest manufacturing companies in America. They had been quick to embrace the new electrical communications technology, which was a fast expanding market, and had taken on the manufacture of telephone equipment, exchanges, switchboards and handsets. These were produced under licence from the Bell Telephone Company which, in 1877, had been founded by Alexander Graham Bell.

At this stage in the story it will be helpful to examine a little of the history of the telephone's development. In so doing it will allow the role of Southgate, a site where much technical innovation occurred, to be set against the backdrop of the rapidly evolving communications technology.

Alexander Graham Bell, who in 1876 had registered his patent for the telephone, had emigrated with his parents in August 1870 from his native Scotland to Canada. His parents, who were concerned for Graham's health, had encouraged him to cross the Atlantic in the hope that a change of climate might improve his chances of survival. The Bells had seen their youngest and oldest sons die of tuberculosis and were fearful that Graham would also succumb to the disease.

Graham Bell had followed in his father's profession, that of teaching the hearing-impaired to speak. By all accounts, Bell senior was a highly competent audiologist. While his father was away in America lecturing, Graham, acting as his assistant, took charge of his London business. When the family eventually moved to Canada, Graham was sent to teach, in place of his father, at a school for the deaf in Boston, Massachusetts. There he remained for three months passing on his knowledge.

During his stay in Boston he made visits to other schools and found that his professional expertise was much in demand. This prompted him to open his own school to enable more teachers to be trained in the use of his techniques. With the idea of improving the way hearing-impaired students learned to speak, Bell developed a method of making speech visible on paper. This visual method he called making a 'photoautograph'.

It has been suggested that the idea of distance communication by converting voice patterns into electrical signals then passing them down wires came to Bell in 1874 when holidaying at his parents' home in Ontario. However, the origins of the idea could have been much further back.

Bell's early education came mostly from his family, although, as a young student, he spent one year at a private school and a further two at the Edinburgh Royal High School from where he graduated at the age of fourteen. Bell also attended some lectures at Edinburgh University and at University College in London. It is possible, while attending the Edinburgh University lectures, that Bell had been made aware of the experiments and invention of the German scientist, Philipp Reis.

In October 1861, Reis had given a demonstration of his invention and also a lecture before the Frankfurt Physical Association entitled 'Telephony by Means of the Galvanic Current'. By some unexplained route one of the Reis telephones arrived at Edinburgh University and it is likely it was there at the time (1862-1863) when Bell was attending lectures at the establishment. It is also known that Bell had studied the work of the eminent scientist Michael Faraday and when in London he had

The telephone system invented by Philipp Reis c.1861— the transmitter is on the left and the receiver on the right.

Alexander Graham Bell's first telephone c.1876.

visited Charles Wheatstone, one of the early pioneers of telegraph communication. It is therefore possible that Bell had already begun to formulate his ideas for the telephone before leaving Britain for Canada.

With his early interests in electrical communication formed probably in the Old World and spurred on by the success of making speech visible in the New World, Bell could no doubt see the opportunity for taking his ideas forward. To do this he would need space to work,

so he set about building a small laboratory in a room above a shop situated at 109 Court Street, Boston.

Bell was well aware that he did not have the necessary technical skills to build good experimental models and he therefore engaged Thomas Watson, a young repair mechanic, as an assistant to help with these tasks. Both men worked well together and soon the years of experimentation and technical thought were brought to a practical conclusion. In March 1876, what has been described as 'the most valuable patent in United States history', patent No.174,465, the telephone, was registered.

Having secured the licence to manufacture telephone equipment, Western Electric employed Clark Muirhead and Company to act as their European agent. Initially, telephone equipment was shipped to Europe from the United States, but it would seem that the pace of market expansion was much too slow for the American company's liking. By the early 1880s Western Electric decided to take direct control of the operation and in 1882 established the first manufacturing facility of its kind in Europe, the Bell Telephone Manufacturing Company of Antwerp. This was followed, in 1883, by the setting-up of a small office in London.

By the late 19th century, with the growth of telephone cable networks in Britain, specialised manufacturers were needed to produce greater quantities of better quality insulated cables to keep pace with other improvements in communications technology. Western Electric, always on the look-out for a business opportunity, had spotted Fowler-Waring Cables, a company situated adjacent to the River Thames at North Woolwich in east London. In the mid-1890s the firm was in financial difficulties which had deterred it from much-needed modernisation. This gave Western Electric the opportunity to buy the company and secure the freehold on the property. The deal was concluded on 1 January 1898 and the site changed hands for £87,000.

By 1910 the area of the North Woolwich site had been doubled with the acquisition of four and a half acres of adjacent land from the Telegraph Construction and Maintenance Company. Although the land was not developed until 1913, Western Electric had wanted to be in a position to respond quickly to future business opportunities which the company thought would soon become available. Their thinking had probably been influenced by the plans of the Government, as in 1912 it had been decided that the Post Office would take over the running of the UK telephone network except for the district around Hull in Yorkshire. Interestingly, Hull has doggedly maintained its independence to this very day.

In their role as the national telephone network provider the Post Office engineers were eager to find ways of cutting costs while improving the quality of communication. The new automatic exchanges, developed in America, seemed the answer as they required fewer operators and the technology was less prone to human error. At the time a number of major suppliers offered the new equipment, most of it made under licence from the American company, Strowger. These were General Electric, Automatic Telephone and Siemens Brothers who were British registered companies. They were also in direct competition with Western Electric.

After the war in Europe (1914-1918) it was important for the British Government to stimulate growth in the UK economy and to create jobs. Therefore, it was felt necessary to spread contracts for the new equipment between the major manufacturers, particularly those who were manufacturing in Britain. At the time it may have been felt that it would be easier for the Post Office to monitor the work of such contractors. Also it would have been easier to ensure that a common technical standard for the new exchanges was implemented and maintained.

Western Electric, on the other hand, would appear to have mis-read the nationalistic signals emanating from Britain after the war. They had planned to manufacture most of their new exchanges at their European plant in Antwerp but with the Post Office's emphasis on manufacture in Britain and with major contracts going to their competitors, they had to change their plans. In 1922 the New Southgate site was secured primarily to manufacture equipment for the Post Office who now had the monopoly of the UK market.

Not long after the setting up of Southgate the facility became famous in the annals of telephone engineering history. After weeks of trials a gathering of several prominent people, including Guglielmo Marconi and representatives of the Post Office and press, came together for what was to become a leap in telephone technology. In the early hours of 15 January 1923, in a wooden hut in the Southgate factory grounds, the visitors were privileged to hear the first one-way transatlantic radio-telephone call, lasting two hours, from America. The wireless technology of Marconi and the telephone technology of Bell had been brought together for the first time.

By the mid-1920s the International Telephone and Telegraph Corporation (ITT) had acquired International Western Electric in a deal which allowed an on-going exchange of patents and access to much technical and manufacturing know-how. However, the agreement only applied outside the United States. The name of the British company changed to Standard Telephones and Cables Limited (STC).

The transatlantic demonstration of 1923 had clearly placed STC in a privileged position, as it was awarded a contract by the Post Office to design and supply long-wave radio-telephone transmitter equipment to be installed at their Rugby facility, the work being completed in 1926. Further contracts for Rugby followed, this time for short-wave transmitters, and it soon became evident that STC were fast becoming recognised as a leading player in the field of global voice communications technology.

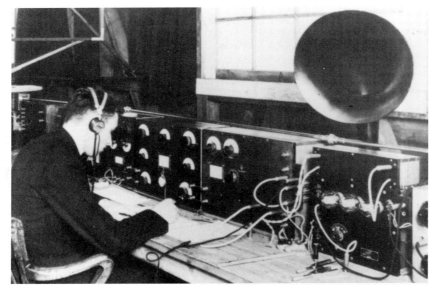

Equipment used for the first one-way Transatlantic telephone call made on 15 January 1923 between New York and New Southgate.

Below. Alec Reeves of STC, the inventor of Pulse Code Modulation (PCM).

With falling charges for telephone calls, brought about in the main by technological improvements, more households wished to be connected to the system and businesses were seeing the advantages of speedy voice communication. This upsurge in demand, particularly for overseas calls, placed greater pressure upon telecommunications engineers to come up with more radical problem solving solutions.

Working in close cooperation with its French associate company, Le Material Telephonique, STC began experiments with the transmission and reception of very short waves in the 17-centimetre range. On 31 March 1931 successful cross-Channel telephone messages were sent and received using parabolic reflectors (dishes) sited at St Margaret's Bay, Kent and at Calais on the French coast. Soon afterwards the electrical press coined the term 'microwave' for this new form of communication.

Over the years many more innovations were to follow. One of the most notable was an early

Telephone switchboards being assembled at the New Southgate factory c.1930. Note how light and spacious this factory was for its day.

form of digital communication called Pulse Code Modulation (PCM). The system was invented by Alec Reeves when he was working in France for the associated STC company, Le Material Telephonique. A patent for the system was filed in France in 1938 and in Britain the following year.

From these early beginnings the world has seen an explosion in the development of microwave and digital technology, not only in the area of telephone calls, but in a whole range of television and multimedia communication.

In 1991 STC was acquired by the multi-national Canadian telecommunications company Nortel (Northern Telecom), giving the engineers at the Southgate site the opportunity to continue providing state-of-the-art global communications solutions and securing a place for this Lea Valley industry in the coming millennium.

REFERENCES

Britannica Micropedia Ready Reference, vol.3 (Chicago, 1992)

Karwatka, Dennis, *Technology's Past* (Prakken Publications Inc., Kentucky, 1996)

Larsen, Egon, *Ideas and Invention* (Spring Books, 1960)

Springate, Stan, *Firm Friends 'Telling it like it was': The Life and Times of STC at New Southgate* (Stan Springate, 1996)

Young, Peter, *Power of Speech—A History of Standard Telephones and Cables 1883-1983* (George Allen & Unwin Ltd., Hertfordshire, 1983)

Note: A device which greatly improved the clarity of telephone speech was the carbon microphone, known as the 'Hunnings Transmitter', invented by Henry Hunnings and patented in Britain on 16 September 1878 and in America on 30 August 1861 (No. 246,512). The design was adopted by the telephone companies and was also widely used in radio communication. Hunnings, a Lea Valley man, was born in Tottenham in 1843, later becoming a clergyman in Yorkshire.

CONSIDERABLE LOCAL INTEREST has persuaded the author to deviate from the original format for this book, with deliberately short chapters, to include a fuller treatment of the beginnings of the Royal Small Arms Factory (RSAF) at Enfield Lock. It is thereby hoped that the reader will be given a greater insight into the site's development during the first half of the 19th century. In setting the scene, it will also be necessary to highlight the various issues which slowed the rate of progress and innovation within the British small arms manufacturing industry in comparison with the speed of technological achievement attained by its American counterpart, particularly in the field of machine tool development. Unfortunately, it will still not be possible to cover in detail the whole range of influences which affected the British small arms industry. However, it is hoped to show that the path of the British small arms industry towards interchangeability and standardised mass produced weapons was anything but straightforward.

Establishing the Armoury

The construction of the small arms factory beside the River Lea at Enfield Lock on the Essex and Middlesex borders came about through a British Government initiative. Action to proceed with construction had been provoked by what the Board of Ordnance regarded as the failure of the private gun trade to provide sufficient quantities of weapons for the British Army and Navy during the Napoleonic Wars. By 1816 the factory and houses for the workmen and their families had been completed. Also during this year the barrel branch from the Royal Manufactory at Lewisham was incorporated into the site as water power for the south London armoury began to fail. The lock and finishing sections from Lewisham were integrated later, adding to the site's gradual expansion. However, it was not until after some forty years of further building and equipping that the Royal Small Arms Factory (as it was to become known)

became capable of producing large quantities of weapons by standardised methods of machine manufacture. Up until the middle of the century the factory acted largely as a research and development establishment, an assembly and small weapon modification shop, and a repair facility. Because of the expert knowledge of arms production and assembly contained within the factory, the establishment was also used to monitor the price and quality of finished parts and complete weapons produced by private contractors for the Board of Ordnance.

Despite the early initiative taken by the British Government to control and secure regular supplies of military small arms by building the factory at Enfield Lock, it took over four decades before regular supplies to the armed forces could be guaranteed from this plant. The circumstances responsible for this somewhat ironic situation

The church at the Royal Small Arms Factory, Enfield Lock was built c.1850, closed in 1922 and demolished in 1928.

The large machine room completed c.1856 with canal, original grinding mill head stream, in the foreground.

provide an interesting study in which it can be shown that the private sector—and not, as commonly believed, the public sector—was still producing the bulk of military small arms up until *c.*1857. Should the reader wish to learn more about the complex series of events which placed the British Government in the embarrassing position of being incapable of providing large quantities of small arms by the middle of the century, the reference section to this chapter is recommended.

THE INFLUENCE OF GEORGE LOVELL
George Lovell was appointed Storekeeper, a position similar to today's General Manager, at Enfield Lock on 1 April 1816, the date coinciding with the barrel branch's move from Lewisham. Most students of the history of the RSAF agree that it was Lovell more than any other individual, who, with his expertise and dedication, laid the foundations and set the bench marks for quality and reliability which were to become synonymous with the RSAF in later years.

Lovell was determined to improve the tolerance standards of weapons and piece parts delivered to 'Ordnance' by the various private contractors. In 1833, armed with a new micrometer, he was able to ascertain that the instruments used for measuring the bores of barrels of small arms varied between 0.752 and 0.760 of an inch. He therefore set the standard at 0.754 of an inch, a measurement which would be strictly adhered to in the future. By necessity, increased levels of accuracy call for greater standards of skill and improved manufacturing techniques if high rejection rates are to be avoided. Improvements of this scale in the short term can lead to a decrease in manufacturing output, accounting for a reduction in profit margins. As might be imagined, Lovell's demands for tolerances to a thousandth of an inch brought considerable criticism from the private contractors. One anonymous observer, unhappy with the new imposed standards, called Lovell 'a cabinet or bedstead maker by trade'. Going on, this nameless person criticised the strictness imposed by the 'Ordnance' viewers (quality control and inspection personnel) upon the private gun trade which led 'to a litigious vexatious nicety of gauging, and finished appearance unknown in the highest finished fowling pieces'. He described as absurd 'the principle of exact jigging, gauging, moulding and other fantastic accuracies'.

Lovell's problems did not subside after his appointment to Inspector of Small Arms in 1840, the most influential position in all aspects of British military weapon design, manufacture, and procurement below that of the Master General of Ordnance. If anything, the personal attacks increased and considerable controversy was to surround his later years. These issues and the consequences of 'Ordnance' imposing strict quality standards form part of the complex nature of the British small arms industry, illustrating the somewhat delicate character of the military gun trade, during the first half of the 19th century.

ORDNANCE'S DILEMMA

It is clear from the many written accounts of the British gun trade in the period to the middle of the 19th century that production was essentially un-cordinated and fragmented, being split mainly between the London and Birmingham private gunmakers. As the demand for arms changed during times of military conflict, the private sector gun manufacturing industry suffered not only from the indecisiveness of Government policies, but also from the general lack of understanding of their needs and requirements by the 'Ordnance' procurement agencies. Skilled men were lost to the industry, sometimes never to return, as many gunmakers were unable to find work for their craftsmen or were denied the stability of long term 'Ordnance' contracts. The apparent reluctance of Government to initiate a policy of major intervention into the arms industry was primarily due to the private gun trade's successful lobby of Parliament, which effectively stopped 'Ordnance' encroaching into their area

The Barrel Room at the Royal Small Arms Factory, Enfield Lock during Mafeking celebrations in 1900.

of business, but was in part due to the strong influence of the Duke of Wellington, who, as Commander in Chief of the Army, believed that arms themselves needed no improvement, the only improvement required being the degree and extent of the troops' instruction in their use.

In addition, the contract system operated by the Board of Ordnance moved from one of favoured manufacturers to one of open tender at the lowest price. This helped create supply and price difficulties for military weapons, as rejection rates increased and contractors tried to recover lost 'Ordnance' business by increasing costs. This helped to deepen the impression that the private sector was incapable of meeting the reasonable demands of 'Ordnance'. As the middle of the century approached, these were just some of the issues facing both 'Ordnance' and the private gun trade.

In October 1853, Mr (later Sir) John Anderson, the chief engineer of the Royal Arsenal at Woolwich, was sent to Enfield, instructed to find out whether the factory was capable of manufacturing bayonets by machinery. Following his visit Anderson issued a report to which the official response of 'Ordnance' was to appoint a Committee to consider the whole question of small arms provision for Her Majesty's Service. Lieutenant Colonel Alexander Tulloh, Royal Artillery, Inspector of the Royal Carriage Factory at Woolwich, and Colonel James Archibald Chalmer, R.A., Inspector of Artillery, reported to the Committee making the following observations:

It appears that the system hitherto adopted to procure small arms is so heterogeneous in its character, that it could not fail to produce considerable difficulties. The Government establishment at Enfield Lock is comparatively small and of a mixed nature, some parts of the work being performed by the establishment, some by contractors; many of the lathes and tools are the property of the workmen; others belonging to the establishment. The men possessing lathes hire them out to other men.

The establishment at Enfield Lock being small, and forming part of the heterogeneous system, is unable to hold that check or control over the contractors to prevent exorbitant demands and serious delays.

The principal part of the gun trade upon which the Government mainly depends for supply in case of emergency, is carried on in Birmingham and London, by men working by hand in wretched cellars and garrets, and great evil arises from the slowness of manufacture.

It can be seen from these findings that the Committee was reinforcing the image, already held by 'Ordnance', that the small arms industry in Britain was in rather a perilous state. This would appear especially true if one considers the imperial role of Britain in the 19th century with the need to police her far-flung Empire. Furthermore, for a nation which had been at the heart of the industrial revolution, it must have been extremely embarrassing for Government to witness senior 'Ordnance' officers being forced to purchase quantities of arms from continental manufacturers in times of conflict. Having to go abroad to find ways of bridging the gaps brought about by recurring delays and non-fulfilment of military contracts by local industry was clearly an unsatisfactory political outcome.

Further scorn was heaped upon the private gun trade when Sir Thomas Hastings, the Ordnance Principal Storekeeper, in evidence to the Committee, read some of the written excuses given by contractors for delays. There were strikes amongst the workmen, difficulty in procuring coal, illness of a skilled artisan, and accident to machinery. It would seem there was little sympathy with the contractors' reasons for delay as Lord Raglan, the Master General of Ordnance, and Sir Thomas Hastings had already formed the view that 'Ordnance' should take control of small arms manufacture. They stated:

> ... they had been guided in their opinion partly by the report of the Commissioners who, during the last year, visited the manufactories of the United States,

The Tool Room at the Royal Small Arms Factory, Enfield Lock during Mafeking celebrations in 1900.

and partly from communications with Mr Anderson and other persons conversant with machinery.

Reading the report, and considering the evidence from the Committee's point of view, it would be difficult to see how they could have reached any other conclusion than for the Board of Ordnance to assume overall responsibility for military small arms manufacture. The past three years had seen a worsening of arms deliveries to 'Ordnance' and the commencement of war in the Crimea had heightened pressure for a radical review of procurement. Given that the British armed forces were again placed in the position of being without sufficient quantities of reliable small arms in time of war, as they had been during the Napoleonic conflict, it might be considered strange that, by the middle of the century, 'Ordnance' still relied heavily upon the independent gun trade for its weapon supplies. The private sector (for reasons explained in the recommended reading) had not modernised its methods of manufacture and did not do so until well into the second half of the century, instead relying heavily on traditional manual skills. Only after their hand had been forced through competition from the new Government factory

at Enfield Lock did the private contractors set up the Birmingham Small Arms company (BSA) in 1861. Further pressure for radical change was heaped on the private sector when 'Ordnance' began placing contracts for weapons manufactured only with interchangeable parts.

DELAYING CHANGE

By 1854 the Board of Ordnance had received from the Commission led by Lt. Colonel Burn, and the previous year Joseph Whitworth (later Sir), reports detailing the fact that the government armouries in America were employing large amounts of machinery in the manufacture of rifles. The level of mechanisation was reported as being particularly advanced in the operations of forming, shaping, and fitting out gun stocks, formerly considered a highly labour intensive part of the gun manufacturing process. It was not as if the American Government was keeping the technology a secret, for machinery capable of making 130 to 160 gun stocks per day was offered to the Board of Ordnance by an American agent Samuel Cox as early as 1841. In fact the technology for manufacturing large-scale irregular and complex shapes in wood had existed in Britain since the early part of the century. Less than one hundred miles from Enfield, in the

The Screw Department at the Royal Small Arms Factory, Enfield Lock during Mafeking celebrations in 1900.

Portsmouth dockyards, the relatively complicated ship's pulley block had been manufactured for the Navy on a sequence of machines invented by Marc Isambard Brunel (father of Isambard Kingdom Brunel) and built by Henry Maudslay, the eminent London engineer. Maudslay's workshops were located within one hour's travel from Enfield, so it is hard to imagine that senior 'Ordnance' personnel were ignorant of the available manufacturing technology, especially as it was the Admiralty, another branch of Government, which had been responsible for financing the Portsmouth block-making factory. However, the process seems not to have been adopted in Britain for the purpose of manufacturing gun stocks although there is evidence which suggests that the principals were probably 'borrowed' by American machine tool inventors and the ideas incorporated into their own designs. These eventually found their way back to Britain via Enfield through the machine tool contract with the Ames Manufacturing Company, Chicopee, Massachusetts, later in the century.

Further examples of differences between British and American manufacturing techniques were observed by 'Ordnance' personnel, prominent engineers, and private small arms contractors at the time of the Great Exhibition of 1851 in London's Hyde Park. Here the American company Robbins and Lawrence had sent six U.S. Army rifles for display and demonstration, all manufactured with parts that interchanged. Samuel Colt exhibited his revolvers which he claimed were made almost entirely by machinery and with interchangeable parts for everyone to see. From the evidence it can be seen that both the Board of Ordnance and the private gun makers were aware of the advances made in machine tool technology on the other side of the Atlantic, yet there was still an apparent reluctance to embrace the processes of mechanisation and mass production. For this reluctance to have existed for so long, it would seem fair to conclude that strong and compelling forces were at play.

GRASPING THE NETTLE

When the second Commission was sent to America in 1854 led by Lt. Colonel Burn R.A, it had been given quite specific instructions to inspect the different gun factories and to purchase such machinery and equipment as found necessary for the proposed new factory at Enfield. This was quite a different approach from that of the Commission of 1853 which included Joseph Whitworth, the distinguished engineer. Whitworth did not go expressly to America to view the gun manufacturers, as might be implied by reading some accounts of the visit. Initially he went to attend the New York Industrial Exhibition. This would indicate that, in less than a year, the procurement of small arms for the British army and navy had reached an extremely

critical state. Accompanied by George Wallis, Headmaster of the Birmingham School of Art, Whitworth appears to have taken it upon himself to alter his itinerary, as it is suggested that 'while there they extended their enquiries by visiting several establishments, among others the Government Arms Factory at Springfield'. This observation is further substantiated in Whitworth's evidence to the 1854 Select Committee when he stated 'that he had not been specially directed to inspect the manufactories of fire-arms, and had not therefore given the close attention to the subject which he would have done if he had foreseen the present inquiry'.

The introduction to the 1854 Committee on Machinery's 87-page report sets out their terms of reference and provides an insight into some of the circumstances which helped bring about a marked change of direction by 'Ordnance'. From the following extract of the report, the reasons can be seen which were eventually to cause 'Ordnance' to take on the responsibility of becoming a major manufacturer of military small arms.

> Owing to the delays constantly recurring in the fulfilment of contracts for arms, the high price demanded by contractors, and the inconvenience occasioned to the Service by these causes, the Honourable Board of Ordnance, towards the end of the year 1853, considered it advisable, in order to secure a regular supply of them, to take this branch of manufacture into their own

hands, and erect a Government establishment capable of producing muskets in large numbers, and at a moderate price by the introduction of machinery into every part of the manufacturing where it was applicable ... Having caused a plan of the building they proposed to erect to be drawn out, ... set to work as speedily as possible; and hearing from Mr Whitworth and others that machinery was extensively applied to this branch of manufacture in the United States of America, were, on account of the high price of labour, the whole energy of people is directed to improving and inventing labour-saving machinery, the Honourable

Board consider it advisable to send over to that country some of their officers, with a view to obtaining every information in their power connected with the manufacture of arms as there conducted, and with the power of buying such machinery as they might consider would be more productive than that used in England for similar purposes.

The second Commission to America placed contracts for machine tools with Robbins & Lawrence of Windsor, Vermont, and the Ames

the American machines in the matter of output etc.

Roberts commented further:-

As regards Messrs. Robbins & Lawrence machines, a small Horizontal Milling Machine of their make, probably one of the last of the plant supplied by them, has been scrapped within the last year or two, although it has not been worked for some time.

From the report of the Commission when

eers and Technical Staff Royal Small Arms Factory, Enfield Lock, 7th December 1918.

Manufacturing Company, Chicopee, Massachusetts. This latter company produced machinery for fashioning gun stocks, bedding the barrel, and letting in the lock. The machinery proved to be so efficient and reliable that, when writing the history of the Royal Small Arms Factory in *c.*1930, G.H. Roberts, the then Superintendent, proudly wrote:

It is interesting to note that several of the woodworking machines supplied by the Ames Co. are still in use today and giving good service, in fact one well known Firm of English machinists recently declared that even today they could not improve upon

visiting the U.S. Armoury at Springfield it would appear that their decision to purchase what must be considered a substantial quantity of machinery was influenced by at least two important factors; that of the sequenced operation of the gun stock forming machinery and the ability of a workman randomly to assemble arms from parts taken from weapons manufactured over a 10-year period. To oversee the installation and the commissioning of the machinery at Enfield Lock, James H. Burton, former Master Armourer of Harpers Ferry Armoury, was brought to England on a five-year contract.

ENFIELD COMES OF AGE

The years 1855 to 1859 saw the rapid expansion of building at Enfield Lock. Construction work was carried out by the Royal Engineers under the supervision of Captain Thomas Bernard Collison, R.E. During this period the large machine room was completed specifically to house the new machinery, much of which was purchased in America by the 1854 Commission. The plant was designed for an estimated annual production of 130,000 muskets and bayonets. In the early years, although expenditure on land, buildings, machinery, and gas works amounted to £315,000, the success of the plant was such that, according to Roberts, by 1862 this sum together with depreciation of £48,000 was said to have been entirely repaid by the reduced cost of production.

Before 1861 the energy source for the Enfield manufactory had been water taken from the River Lea to drive two 18-foot diameter cast-iron water wheels, each having an estimated output of 46hp. The design of the drive, which did not incorporate governors, was reported to have made the outputs very irregular. Primarily the main function of the water wheels was to run the barrel grinding shop which, according to reports, continued with this source of power until 1887. Amazingly it has been recorded that the use of the traditional grit grindstone was not finally discontinued until c.1926.

In 1852 a new Barrel Rolling Plant was installed and by 1853 Roberts reported that the factory capacity was 50,000 muskets and 3,000 swords per annum. Prior to this, and using only an average of 25 horse power before steam was introduced, it was claimed that the production rate of the Enfield factory had been in the order of 7,000 small arms and 1,500 swords annually. However, Professor Tim Putnam, an historian of industrial technology, when referring to George Lovell, suggests that 'the number of complete weapons in his period never approached that figure'. This, he concludes, is based upon the assumption that Enfield was using a number of individual components purchased from the private contractors rather than manufacturing the complete arm in-house.

Once the American machine tools had been installed at Enfield, not only was there a dramatic increase in arms production, but their introduction made the RSAF the first British plant to be able to claim that their machined parts were so accurate that they could be interchanged between weapons. This is the first true example of a British factory using mass production techniques, as defined by the manufacture of standardised machine made parts that interchanged completely, rather than those which are made to fit on an individual basis, usually by hand finishing. The new system of manufacture was so successful that by the year ending 30 June 1860 the output of rifles alone had increased to 90,707, an average of 1,744 per week, later to go up to 1,900. By the year 1861, 1,700 men were employed at the plant and it is recorded that the large machine room (currently the Grade II listed building with the clock tower)

The view, facing north, showing remains of old grinding machines after excavation in building No. 86, later designated building No.64.

The remains of old grinding machines, excavated in 1968, showing castings placed in them before the floor was boarded over in 1914/1918.

military weapons with standardised and interchangeable parts by the extensive use of machine tools.

In this chapter a number of issues have been highlighted which have arisen out of the installation of the 'American system' at Enfield Lock. Should the reader wish to gain a deeper knowledge of the complexities surrounding the British small arms industry in the 19th century, an analysis, together with the effects, problems, and advantages for both the Board of Ordnance and the independent gun trade, can be derived from the recommended reading.

The Royal Small Arms Factory at Enfield Lock lasted for over 170 years, providing arms for the Allied forces in two World Wars. Many of the famous Lee Enfield magazine rifles can still be seen in use around the world today. This is a lasting tribute to the quality of the product produced by the RSAF workforce. It was a sad day for manufacturing in the Lea Valley when the factory closed in August 1987.

During its life the factory created work for generations of local people, in many cases whole families. It has often been said that once you had served an apprenticeship or had been employed at the RSAF then your skills would be in great demand from other employers.

REFERENCES

Bailey, De Witt, 'George Lovell and The Growth of the RSAF Enfield', paper presented at MA Day School, Middlesex University, 4th July 1992

Blackmore, Howard L., 'Military Gun Manufacturing in London and the Adoption of Interchangeability', *Arms Collecting*, vol.29, no.4 (November 1991)

Cottesloe, Colonel, Lord, CB, 'Notes on the History of the Royal Small Arms Factory, Enfield Lock', *Army Historical Research*, vol.12 (undated, probably c.1932)

Gilbert, K.R., 'The Ames Recessing Machine: A Survivor Of The Original Enfield Rifle Machinery', *Technology and Culture*, vol.4, part 2, 1963

House of Lords Record Office, London, *Report of the Committee on the Machinery of the United States of America*, presented to the House of Commons, in Pursuance of their Address of 10 July 1855

Institute of Civil Engineers—Minutes of Proceedings,

was driven by two 40hp steam engines with Fairbairn expansion gear, while in the barrel mill a 70 horse power steam engine was employed along with the existing water wheels.

It would therefore seem that one could proclaim with confidence that the 'American system of manufactures' (as it has popularly become known) had truly arrived at Enfield and was seen to be working. The private gun trade had yet to respond to the challenge of producing vol.27, 'Address of the President', C.H. Gregory (London, 1867-1868)

Putnam, Tim & Weinbren, Dan, *A Short History of the Royal Small Arms Factory Enfield* (Middlesex University, 1992)

Report from the Select Committee on Small Arms (House of Commons, May 1854) 184. 251

Royal Ordnance, Nottingham, 'Notes on the History of the Royal Small Arms Factory, Enfield Lock', unsigned typed manuscript *c.*1930, accompanied by a memorandum, dated 24/12/30, signed, G.H. Roberts (Superintendent RSAF 1922-1931), clearly showing that he is the author of the RSAF history.

Whitworth, J. & Wallis, G., *The Industry of the United States in Machinery, Manufacturers and Useful and Ornamental Arts* (1854)

NOTES:

1. There does appear to be some confusion with regard to the actual date when the RSAF was first established. R.H.Roberts in his notes suggests the establishment was, 'about the year 1804'. Colonel Lord Cottesloe, C.B. confirms this date in his article, 'Notes on the History of the Royal Small Arms Factory, Enfield Lock', vol.12 of *Army Historical Research*. This is not particularly surprising as Cottesloe bases most of his article on the notes of Roberts. In A. Robinson's and J. Burnby's Occasional Paper no.50 for the Edmonton Hundred Historical Society, 'Guns and Gun Powder in Enfield', it suggests that negotiations were started for the land to build the new manufactory on 14 July 1811. George Lovell (appointed as Storekeeper at Enfield Lock, 1 April 1816), in his report on the background and present state of the Enfield factory (W.O.44/682) to Sir Henry Hardinge (Board of Ordnance) lists the following under 'Lands': '4 Acres, 2 Rods, 5 Poles of Sedgy and Swampy Ground adjoining the River, purchased therewith from William Sotherby, Esq. in 1808.'

2. There has been some confusion as to who actually led the 1854 Commission on Machinery during their American tour. For example, David A. Hounshell, in his book, *From the American System to Mass Production 1800-1932: The Development of Manufacturing Technology in the United States* (The John Hopkins University Press, Baltimore, 1984, p.4), suggests that John Anderson was the leader. However, it is clear from the *Report of the Committee on the Machinery of the United States of America*, presented to the House of Commons, in Pursuance of their Address of the 10 July 1855 (House of Lords Record Office, London, p.2 [548]) that Anderson was not the leader. Here it is clearly documented that Lieutenant Colonel Burn, Royal Artillery, who held the position of Assistant Inspector of Artillery at Woolwich, had been appointed to lead the Commission. A communication dated 13 February 1854,

from the Office of Ordnance shows that the Secretary to the Board of Ordnance, J. Wood, had passed on the Board's instruction to Burn stating, 'I am to add that Lieutenant Warlow, Royal Artillery, and Mr. Anderson, have been instructed to proceed thither on the 4th March next, and to place themselves under your direction; and I am to request you will give them such instructions previous to your departure as you may consider necessary'.

Interestingly, in the unpublished history of the RSAF written by G.H. Roberts he mistakenly lists a Major Turborville accompanying Lt. Colonel Burn, Lieutenant Warlow and Mr Anderson as part of the Commission sent to America in 1854. All the documentary evidence which includes the Report of the Committee on the Machinery of the United States of America, lists only the latter three members. In fact this report, which describes their findings during the tour of American manufacturing establishments in 1854 and was presented to the House of Commons, 'in Pursuance of their Address of the 10th July, 1855', is signed only by Burn, Warlow and Anderson.

Roberts' mistake is curious as he clearly had access to material which may not have been freely available to other historians at the time. In the preface to his 'Notes on the History of the Royal Small Arms Factory, Enfield Lock', he states 'The writer wishes to place on record his indebtedness to Sir Herbert J. Creedy, Secretary of the War Office, for permission to consult a number of War Office records'.

Apart from this one transgression, Roberts is to be congratulated for having the interest and enthusiasm to begin assembling the facts which have assisted later historians with their researches into the history of the RSAF.

3. The possible explanation for Lovell being called a 'bedstead maker', is that in the late 1820s, to keep the Enfield factory going, Lovell took on all kinds of work, including making bedsteads.

It is worth noting that George Lovell, the first Storekeeper at the RSAF, should not to be confused with Frederick Lovell, his brother, Clerk 1824, or Francis George Lovell, his son, Assistant Inspector of Arms 1843. Robert Lovell, another son, also worked in the industry.

4. For further reading and an in-depth study of the reasons which delayed the introduction of weapons made with interchangeable parts see PhD Thesis by James H. Lewis, 'The Development of the Royal Small Arms Factory (Enfield Lock) and its Influence Upon Mass Production Technology and Product Design *c.*1820-*c.*1880'. Copies of the thesis can be viewed by appointment at Middlesex University, Tottenham Campus Library, White Hart Lane, London N17 8HR, or the Ministry of Defence Pattern Room, The Enfield Building, Kings Meadow Road, Nottingham NG2 1EQ.

Who Put the Lee in the 'Lee-Enfield Rifle'?

IF YOU were to ask the average citizen of Enfield what made the town famous, the probable answer would be the Lee-Enfield Rifle. While it is true that the Pattern 1853 series rifle was the first British weapon to have the distinction of being named after a town (Enfield), the name Lee did not arrive on the scene until much later in the century and had nothing to do with either the river or the valley.

The Pattern 1853, a muzzle loader, first saw service with the British Army in the Crimean War (1853-1856) but did not go into full-scale production until January 1857. Muzzle loaders had distinct disadvantages for the soldier in the heat of battle as the ball and charge had to be rammed down the barrel with a rod (ramrod). This meant it was necessary for the soldier to stand upright to accomplish the task, presenting the enemy with a simple target.

By the 1860s muzzle loading had become old technology as the method of breech loading increased in popularity. However, there were substantial stocks of the Enfield pattern 1853 held by the British Army after the Crimean War and it made economic sense to have them converted to the new Snider breech loading system. Apart from the improved way of loading,

the Snider had also been designed to accept the revolutionary rolled brass cartridge developed by Colonel Boxer at Woolwich. Now it was possible for the soldier to load his weapon with comparative ease and safety, while lying prone on the ground.

The decision to use Snider's method of converting the Pattern 1853 had been arrived at through open competition. In August 1864, following the recommendations of the Committee on Breech Loading Arms, the War Office issued an advertisement inviting gunmakers and inventors to submit plans to convert the Enfield pattern 1853 from a muzzle loader to a breech-loader, calling for two main criteria to be met. Firstly, the cost was 'not to exceed £1 per arm' and, secondly, it was a requirement that 'The shooting of the converted arm [should] not be inferior to the Enfield rifle' (un-modified muzzle loader). On completion of the modifications the weapons were to be assessed for accuracy, penetration, initial velocity, recoil, rapidity of fire, liability to failure, simplicity of management, fouling and exposure to weather.

The advertisement attracted 50 applicants for the work, which after careful examination

Lee Enfield Rifle 0.303" SMLE (MkIII).

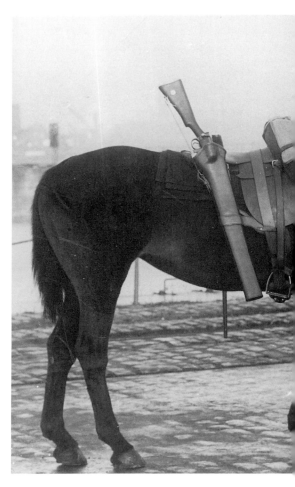

Cavalry soldier at docks with horse (c.1914). Note the 0.303" Short, Magazine Lee Enfield Rifle in its specially designed holster, which was part of the standard equipment carried by the horse.

were whittled down to the eight most promising candidates. Over the coming months extensive trials were carried out when it was reported that more than 5,500 rounds were fired with only one mis-fire. This not only gave the Committee faith in the breech-loading system, but also the confidence to recommend the Snider method of conversion.

Over the years, the improved weapon was to go through a long evolutionary process when different inventors' systems were tried—Martini-Henry, Enfield-Martini, Lee-Burton, Lee-Metford, to name but a few. However, the War Office placed great emphasis on a design which would always function reliably under the severest of battlefield conditions (exposure to weather and mud). In 1895 the forerunner of the weapon, which was to serve the Allied Forces throughout two World Wars and beyond, eventually emerged. This was the highly acclaimed Lee-Enfield Magazine Rifle Mk.1. But what about the connection with the name Lee, I hear you ask?

James Paris Lee was born in Hawick, Scotland in August 1831. In 1836 his family emigrated to Canada where he grew up and developed an interest in firearms. After serving an apprenticeship in his father's clock and watchmaking business he moved to Ontario where he set up on his own account in 1850. While there he married Caroline Chrysler (an early relative of the now famous car manufacturer). In 1860, with the addition of two sons, Lee moved with his family to Wisconsin in America. Here he experimented with a range of his own and some standard weapons, converting the famous Springfield muzzle loader to a breech loading system in 1861.

Lee persevered with his obsession of

James Paris Lee (1831-1904).

creating a repeating weapon and, after years of experimentation and carrying out work for two of America's famous weapons companies, Sharp and Remington, his ideas for a bolt action magazine rifle were taken up by the British War Office. Manufacture of the now internationally famous Lee-Enfield Rifle commenced at the Royal Small Arms Factory, Enfield Lock in 1895.

Amazingly, the later Mk.4 version of the Lee-Enfield can still be seen in use around the world today. This is not only a lasting tribute to Lee, but it is an acknowledgement of the engineering skills of the Lea Valley workforce who, over the years, produced this weapon in vast quantities.

REFERENCES

Lewis, James H., 'The Development of the Royal Small Arms Factory (Enfield Lock) and its Influence Upon

James Paris Lee (1831-1904) seated next to his brother, John, from whose foundry, in Wallaceberg Ontario, the first Lee rifle was said to have been fired.

JAMES PARIS LEE 1831-1904

One of the foremost 19th century arms inventors, Lee was born in Scotland. In 1836 his family came to Canada and settled at Galt. Lee was trained in his father's profession of watchmaker and jeweller, before moving to Wisconsin about 1858, where he began his career as an inventor. His greatest contribution to firearms design was made in 1878 when he completed the development of the "box magazine". Tradition holds that this occurred at Wallaceburg while Lee was visiting his brother John, a local foundry owner. The magazine was first incorporated in his U.S. Navy rifle of 1879. Eight years later his rifle was adopted by the British Army and, with modifications, it became, in 1895, the Lee-Enfield, which remained a standard British weapon for over sixty years.

Erected by the Ontario Heritage Foundation,
Ministry of Culture and Recreation

A plaque erected by the Ontario Heritage Foundation, close to the site of the John Lee foundry in Queen Elizabeth Municipal Park, on the north side of the Sydenham River, to commemorate the claim that James Paris Lee fired the first shot from his prototype rifle, in 1879, into an oak plank on the opposite bank.

Mass Production Technology and Product Design *c.1820-c.1880'*, unpublished PhD thesis, Middlesex University, December 1996

Skennerton, Ian D., *The Lee Enfield Story* (Ian D. Skennerton, Australia, 1993)

House of Lords Record Office, London. Subject: The Trials of nine descriptions of Breech-loading Rifles accepted for competition in accordance with the terms of the War Office Advertisement of 22/10/66. Reference, Reports Commissioners 1886-68, XVI, pp.32-34

Notes:

1. The Enfield Pattern 1853 rifle was the first weapon in Britain to be made under the mass production system using interchangeable parts.

2. By 1856 the War Office was responsible for weapon procurement for the armed forces. Formerly this role had been performed by the Board of Ordnance.

CHARLES BABBAGE, the son of a banker, was born near Teignmouth in Devon on 26 December 1792. It has been suggested that Babbage was a sickly child and received a 'desultory' education, first at a private school near Exeter, and later at his father's old school, King Edward VI Grammar School at Totnes, Devon. Here, along with other boys, Charles was given a classical education. The school was located in a 17th-century building which was cold and draughty during the winter months. This hostile environment did not suit the young Babbage's poor health and as a consequence he was taken out of school. He then spent the following two years at home being taught, not very effectively by all accounts, by private tutors.

Towards adolescence, Babbage's health began to improve and he was sent to the school of the Rev. Stephen Freeman at Enfield, Middlesex, where he remained for three years. The school, which has been described as 'a large brick house, at the upper end of Baker Street', was the residence of a Mr. R.C. Middleton in the early part of this century. According to the *History of Enfield* by Cuthbert Wilfrid Whitaker, the house was called Homewood and was 'approached through a splendid wrought iron gate'.

Charles Babbage, FRS (1792-1871).

The early years of Babbage's schooling allow us glimpses of the lad's enquiring mind. For example, he investigated popular schoolboy beliefs of the day, particularly those dealing with life after death and the supernatural. To prove or disprove the existence of the Devil, he engaged in such acts as going into an empty room at dusk, cutting his finger and with the blood drawing a circle on the floor. Then he stood inside the circle and repeated the Lord's Prayer backwards. This was one of the ways his peers believed that Beelzebub could be summoned.

To discover if life existed after death, he made a pact with a school friend that the first of them to die would somehow return to make a sign to the other. Babbage's friend later joined the Navy and after returning from a particularly arduous Mediterranean tour, he contracted tuberculosis and died at the age of eighteen. Babbage's preparations on the night of his friend's death demonstrate his logical approach. Before going to bed, Babbage made sure that no bird or animal had entered his room which, if gone unnoticed, might have caused him to reach a wrong conclusion. He also paid particular attention to the furniture and other objects in his room, presumably to check if, through positioning or change, attempts were being made to contact him. After Babbage had spent a '… night of perfect sleeplessness' it would appear that the only sounds which disturbed the silence were those of a '… distant clock and a faithful dog, just outside [his] door …'.

While at school in Enfield, Babbage began to develop his mathematical skills. The school had a library with over 300 volumes, including a treatise on algebra, and a copy of Ward's *Young*

Approached through the wrought-iron gate is the school of the Reverend Stephen Freeman at Enfield, where Charles Babbage attended as a youth. The building once stood at the north end of Baker Street near the junction with Clay Hill where a line of 1930s-style houses now stands.

Mathematician's Guide, a book which Babbage acknowledged in later life to have been influential in developing his interest in the subject.

A clue to Babbage's analytical development and an early indication of his blossoming genius came from his ability to solve problems. At the time it was common for the older boys at the school to make cyphers. It would seem that the young Babbage was able to discover the key to these puzzles quite easily, which did not make him popular with the senior boys. He was sometimes bullied for showing that he was intellectually superior to them.

In October 1810, two months before his 19th birthday, Babbage entered Trinity College, Cambridge. He graduated in 1814 and in 1817 he took an M.A. During his time at Cambridge, around 1812, Babbage began to develop his ideas of how to calculate numerical tables mechanically. Between 1820 and 1822 he constructed a machine with a series of wheels which were integrated in such a way that the calculation was performed on the principle of difference.

Imagine a simple mechanical device having three wheels, each having 10 numbered teeth and each wheel connected to the other in such a way as to influence movement at the required time. Now imagine wheel one making 10 revolutions, then moving wheel two forward by one tooth. Therefore, wheel two has calculated that wheel one has revolved 10 times. If wheel two is made to move through one complete revolution it would have calculated that wheel one has revolved 100 times and wheel three would have moved forward once. It can also be seen that the movements of the numbered wheels act as a memory store. By constructing a machine with several hundred numbered wheels which are related mathematically, one to another, other calculations can now be performed.

It will be appreciated that, with the machine tools and hand finishing of the day, it was a laborious task to achieve the accuracies required to make Babbage's Difference and Analytical Engines. In fact Babbage devoted 37 years of his life and much of his personal finances into perfecting such devices, incorporating punch-card type systems with ideas borrowed from the Jacquard loom. One might speculate on how computing science would have developed had Babbage not had his mathematical appetite whetted at a small private school situated at Enfield in the Lea Valley.

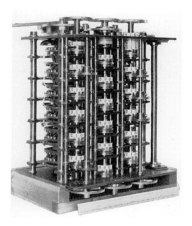

A reproduction, showing part of a working Babbage 'Difference Engine', which was constructed from the original in the Science Museum, London. The apparatus was the practical outcome of Babbage's early experiments.

The Science Museum in London has a working model of a Babbage Difference Engine weighing about three tonnes, which was built in 1991 to commemorate the bicentenary of Babbage's birth.

REFERENCES

Mosley, Maboth, *Irascible Genius—A Life Of Charles Babbage, Inventor* (Hutchinson & Co., 1964)
Russell, Eric, 'Babbage's Engines', *Electronics Times* (London, 27 October 1997)
Stephen, Leslie & Lee, Sidney (eds.), *Dictionary of National Biography*, vol.1 (Smith & Elder, 1908)

Note: The reader may wish to consult the next chapter which deals with R.W. Munro, the precision engineering firm which was located at Bounds Green, north London, and the connections with Charles Babbage.

It is known that Babbage sent his sons to the Rowland Hill School at Bruce Castle when it was being run by Hill's younger brother, Arthur. This would suggest that there were at least three connections between Babbage and the Lea Valley.

STRANGE as it may seem the firm of R.W. Munro, located in the north London suburb of Bounds Green, had connections with two of the world's most famous names in computer science, Babbage and IBM.

Robert William Munro (1839-1912) had originally worked with his elder brother James in the trade of their father, a mathematical and optical instrument maker, in the London borough of Lambeth. It would appear that, after working together for a short time, the two brothers parted amicably, James to manufacture machine tools and Robert to set up in business on his own account. In 1864 Robert Munro founded a company which was to become recognised internationally for setting standards of excellence in precision engineering.

The standard of Munro's work and the variety of products quickly established the company as a quality manufacturer with a number of influential clients. As Munro's reputation grew, prestigious contracts arrived from government departments, scientific bodies and The Bank of England. To maintain the quality of engineering as the business began to expand, Munro, in 1867, took on a young engineer, Francis John Rooker, a graduate of Birkbeck College, London. This decision has been recognised by those within the industry as an example of Munro's clear judgement of character.

R.W. Munro, with his early workforce, seen on the extreme left of second row. On Munro's left is F.J. Rooker who became one of the Company's most respected and long serving engineers. The picture was taken in 1884 outside the Granville Works, Kings Cross, London.

The founder Robert William Munro, F.R.Met.Soc. (1839-1912).

Francis John Rooker who joined the firm of R.W. Munro in 1867 and remained until his retirement in 1932, a total of 65 years' service.

On this occasion Munro seems to have surpassed himself, as Rooker went on to serve the company until his retirement in 1932, a total of 65 years, by which time he had made many major contributions to much of the product design and development.

Throughout Munro's life he had taken more than a passing interest in the science of meteorology; in fact, he was elected to fellowship of the Royal Meteorological Society. Munro's interest, coupled with his skills as an instrument maker, no doubt gained him important contacts within the field of meteorology. In the early years this would have helped to promote and establish his business.

Following the Tay Bridge disaster in 1879, which was attributed to severe wind conditions, The Meteorological Committee appointed W.A. Dines to undertake research into ways of accurately measuring wind force. Munro received a commission to work with Dines and in 1892 the first anemometer was produced. The instrument, the Dines' pressure tube anemometer, which was eventually accepted as a universal standard, was installed at the home of Dines where it was said still to have been working accurately over seventy years later.

Due to the anemometer's success many orders were placed with Munro for installation in meteorological stations in Britain and abroad. When Captain Robert Falcon Scott commanded the second British Antarctic expedition in 1910, a Dines' anemometer, suitably modified to protect against ice and snow, was loaned for the occasion. It was reported in a very matter-of-fact way that the instrument was 'a great success in practice'.

Following the return of the anemometer, it was further modified by Rooker who incorporated a direction recorder of his own design into the instrument, before it accompanied Sir Ernest Shackleton on his 1914 Antarctic expedition. Unfortunately the instrument, which had been installed on the supply ship *Endurance*, was lost when the ship became trapped and crushed by the ice.

In later years pressure tube anemometers were to become standard equipment with many respected bodies, such as the United Nations Organisation, the British Atomic Energy Authority and the Air Ministry. Orders from many of these organisations were placed with R.W. Munro Ltd.

In 1870, with an order book increasing in size, Munro moved from his works in Bridgewater Gardens to larger premises at Clerkenwell Green in the east end of London. In six years he had outgrown these premises and in 1876 a further move was found necessary to even larger work-space at Granville Place, Kings Cross. Here Munro remained for 29 years, producing a range of precision instruments from

A bank-note printing and numbering machine constructed by R.W. Munro for the Bank of England c.1880.

The Munro premises in Cornwall Road, Tottenham, London, N15 were first occupied by the firm in 1905. In 1938 a move was made to a new single-storey factory, purpose built, in Cline Road, Bounds Green, London, N11.

seismographs to hydrographic equipment to printing presses for The Bank of England. However, by 1905 the firm was forced by expansion to move once more to new premises at Cornwall Road, Tottenham, where it remained until 1938. The final move in that year was to a large modern factory in Cline Road, Bounds Green, now in the London Borough of Haringey.

It was at the Bounds Green site in 1956, at this time jointly run by Alfred James Munro (eldest son of the founder) and Robert Clarke Munro (second son of the founder), that an order was received from IBM for a working reproduction of a section of Charles Babbage's Difference Engine, a model of which existed in the Science Museum at Kensington. If the order could be completed, IBM wished to display the exhibit, an important part of computing history, in their Watson Research Laboratory at Yorktown, in the United States. The Munro company rose to the challenge, and under the direction of Ivor Harding, the then head of the design office, painstaking research, analysis, measurement and drawing of the Science

Museum model finally resulted in a working replica.

The IBM challenge was one which could hardly have been refused by the second generation of Munros, since in 1880 Major General H.P. Babbage (son of Charles), who had inherited much of his late father's unfinished work, had requested Robert William Munro to manufacture the components for the construction of 'The Mill', part of the original Analytical Engine.

Here once more is an example of a company which strenuously maintained a tradition of excellence in precision engineering for over one hundred years and which had chosen to locate its business in the Lea Valley, drawing upon, and adding to, the skills of local people.

REFERENCES

Author unknown, *R.W. Munro Ltd.—Centenary, 1864-1964* (R.C. Munro Ltd., 1964)

Lee, Sidney (ed.), *Dictionary of National Biography*, vol.18 (Smith Elder & Co, 1909)

J.A. Prestwich—Tottenham's Prolific Inventor

JOHN ALFRED PRESTWICH was born on 1 September 1874 in Kensington, London. The family appear to have moved to Warmington House in Tottenham High Road a little before the boy's 14th birthday. Here John's father continued his business as a photographer, which probably explains why the lad took an early interest in moving picture technology, at the time in an early stage of development.

At school young Prestwich is said to have acquired a good understanding of mathematics and draughtsmanship which gained him two scholarships, one to the City and Guilds School and the other to the City of London School. It is also said that he showed an early aptitude for things mechanical, building his first model steam engine by the age of fourteen. On leaving school at the age of 16, Prestwich went to work for the Ferranti company, which at the time was producing electrical equipment and scientific instruments at premises at Aldgate in the east end of London. By the age of 18, Prestwich had moved to a firm engaged in the manufacture of heavy engineering work, from locomotives to wood-carving machines.

However, it seems that Prestwich was unable to contain his enthusiasm for developing his own ideas and in 1895, at the age of 20, he set up on his own account as the Prestwich Manufacturing Company, making electrical fittings and scientific instruments, in a greenhouse at his father's Tottenham home.

As the moving picture craze hit Britain in the late 19th century, Prestwich was able to combine his earlier photographic knowledge with his considerable engineering skills to produce a range of equipment for the burgeoning industry.

From early sales brochures it can be seen that Prestwich's output was prolific. He invented, designed and manufactured cameras, printers, projectors, machines for perforating, measuring and cutting film. He also became expert at the art of making and showing films. This no doubt got the young man noticed, as for a brief period he entered into partnership with the inventor of Britain's cinematograph (there were several other countries, America, France and Germany claiming the prize) William Friese-Greene. On 21 June 1889 Friese-Greene had filed his patent,

William Friese-Greene (1855-1921), the first Briton to produce moving pictures on a celluloid film, who for a time had formed a company in partnership with J.A. Prestwich.

A Prestwich motion picture camera on Captain Scott's Antartic Expedition of 1910.

No.10,131, for 'a camera for producing a series of photographic images in rapid succession upon a celluloid film'.

Although Prestwich continued with his photographic business for almost twenty years, he was unable to resist his first real love, that of designing and making engines. Prior to his marriage in 1898 to Elinor Bramley, he had acquired 1 Landsdown Road, Tottenham for his workshop and he now took up residence next door, at no.3, with his new bride.

It was not long before the growing success of the business required extra space and Prestwich was fortunate to acquire a disused chapel next to 1 Landsdown Road. By 1903, with a workforce of 50, it was possible for Prestwich to produce commercially a motor-cycle engine which he had begun designing sometime earlier. The 293cc J.A.P. engine was incorporated by the Triumph Cycle Company of Birmingham into one of their machines. At the time the motor-cycle industry was going through an uncertain phase in the

John Alfred Prestwich (1874-1952), founder of the Company.

Below. *J.A. Prestwich & Company's early premises in Landsdown Road, Tottenham (c.1900). Part of the building is currently (1999) occupied by a health clinic.*

Right. *A view of approximately half of the capstan lathe bay of the J.A.P. Northumberland Park factory c.1950. At the time there were 19 bays of machinery in operation.*

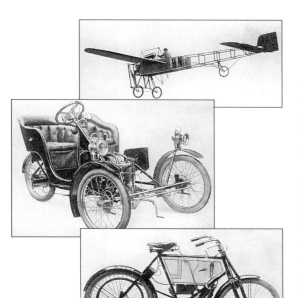

vehicle's popularity. However, the J.A.P. engine, which was made to exacting standards, was reported to be so reliable that its introduction was said to have founded the motor-cycle industry in Britain.

Between 1903 and 1909 J.A.P. manufactured not only motor-cycle engines but complete machines and even experimented with early motor car construction. It was a J.A.P. engine which powered the historic flight of A.V. Roe's triplane on 13 July 1909, when it became the first all British aircraft to fly with a British pilot. For a time Prestwich and Roe were in partnership, forming the J.A.P. Avro-plane Company, but this enterprise was short-lived. Not long after Roe's flight, Prestwich saw his own monoplane built at his factory and fly from the Tottenham marshes, piloted by H.J. Harding, a local aeronautical enthusiast who had collaborated in the project.

As motor-cycling gained popularity with the general public, demand for engines increased. No doubt the pressure to produce more engines had been partially provoked by J.A.P. itself through a policy, which had been adopted some years earlier, of not competing directly with customers by producing complete motor-cycles. It had also been decided to stop aircraft engine production and to concentrate the manufacturing effort on the popular motor-cycle engine.

Production at Landsdown Road had long outstripped the small workshop's capacity and in January 1911 manufacturing was transferred to a new plant in Northumberland Park, Tottenham which had been designed for future expansion. The move was to prove timely as, during the lead-up to the First World War, the British Government had begun to increase the level of

From top.

The J.A.P. monoplane flying over Tottenham marshes in 1909.

The J.A.P. 'Dual Car' fitted with a 4.5 HP engine, 1905.

An example of an early (1908) J.A.P. production motorcycle. There were several earlier models.

A Speedway racing bike c.1950 with a J.A.P. 500cc engine. The sport of Speedway became very popular after the Second World War with many teams competing in a league system. J.A.P. had a monopoly of this market.

A Cooper light racing car powered by a J.A.P. 500cc engine c.1950.

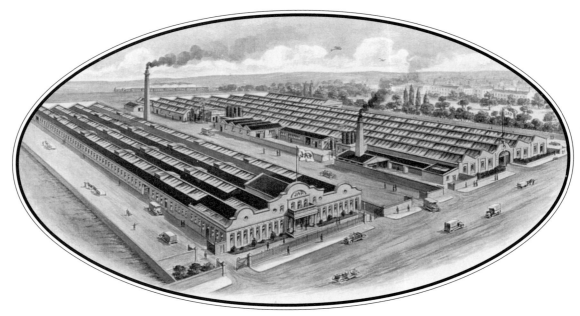

An artist's impression of J.A. Prestwich & Company's Northumberland Park factory, c.1915.

contracts placed with the company. These were for various types of munitions, aircraft parts and motor-cycle engines. As the war progressed and skilled men left the factory to join the conflict, women were employed on the production work.

At the cessation of hostilities, business for J.A.P. dramatically increased as former German customers returned and placed annual orders for 35,000 engines. In the post-war period new racing engines were designed to keep J.A.P. in the forefront of motor-cycle technology. Like many companies, J.A.P. suffered during the depression of the late 1920s and early 1930s but was saved by the tenacity of its owner and by adopting a flexible manufacturing policy.

A turning point in J.A.P.'s lagging fortune came in the years leading up to the Second World War with the development of a portable, air-cooled, industrial petrol engine. The launch of this design could not have come at a better time for Britain or J.A.P. and, with the introduction of a new water-cooled engine to take on heavier work, the company was able to provide some 240,000 units in support of the war effort. These highly reliable engines performed numerous tasks all over the world; powering tractors, pumping water, driving machinery and generating electricity; their different uses would

appear almost countless. As in the First World War J.A.P. manufactured munitions and other equipment on a huge scale for the allied forces, producing some 10 million time and percussion fuses, 23 million small contact fuses and in excess of five and a quarter million aircraft parts. This was apart from engine and other production.

Although J.A.P. prospered directly after the war and made several innovative contributions to engine design, as with many other Lea Valley companies in the early 1960s, the firm was forced to succumb to increasing pressure, brought about in the main by overseas competition. The North-umberland Park factory finally closed its gates on 21 August 1963. However, there is no doubt that John Alfred Prestwich through his pioneering work and dedication to excellence, over many years, had helped perfect the mass-production of a range of affordable, reliable and versatile engines which had a marked effect on the quality of life of many people throughout the world.

REFERENCES

Buchanan, D.J., *The J.A.P. Story, 1895-1951* (J.A. Prestwich, Northumberland Park, Tottenham, 1951)

Clew, Jeff, *J.A.P.—The Vintage Years* (Haines Publishing Group, Yeovil, 1985)

Clew, Jeff, *J.A.P.—The End of an Era* (Haines Publishing Group, Yeovil, 1988)

A.V. Roe—The Lea Valley Flyer

THE ENGINEER and aviator Edwin Alliott Verdon Roe (he preferred to be called Alliott) was born on 26 April 1877 at Patricroft near Manchester. He first became interested in flight while serving in the Merchant Navy. On a voyage in 1902 he watched a soaring albatross which afterwards inspired him to build and experiment with a variety of model aircraft, some of which he displayed at the 1906 and 1907 Motor and Aeronautical Shows held in the Agricultural Hall, Westminster, London.

As interest in aviation grew in Britain the *Daily Mail* newspaper offered cash prizes for models weighing between two and fifty pounds (1-22kg) capable of flying above the height of fifty feet (15.2m). In 1907 Roe won the highest awarded prize of £75 for the flight of his 9ft. 6in. (2.85m) wing-span model in a competition held at Alexandra Palace, Wood Green, North London. Although the amount of money was meagre, in relation to supporting future experimental and development work, the prize won by Roe's rubber powered entry no doubt encouraged him to pursue his ambitious plans.

In 1908 Roe formed his first serious business partnership with the now famous Tottenham engineer, J.A. Prestwich, with capital of £100, but their J.A.P. Avroplane Company was short-lived, lasting little over one year.

To raise the finance required for further development and experimentation, Roe borrowed from both his father and brother Humphrey. The latter owned a factory in Manchester manufacturing trouser braces under the trade name 'Bulls Eye'. In gratitude for the financial support given by his brother, Roe displayed the name 'Bulls Eye' on his triplane. A partnership with Humphrey culminated in the formation, in 1910, of the now more familiar A.V. Roe and Company.

Under the new partnership Humphrey was responsible for all matters of finance and management, allowing Alliott to concentrate his engineering skills on aircraft design. However, it would appear that under this new arrangement Humphrey wanted much closer control of operations, so a workshop was established in the factory of Evershead & Co. at Ancotes, Manchester, which allowed him to keep a close rein on the business. The arrangement saw aircraft, built in Manchester, transported south for flight testing at Brooklands, Surrey.

Roe built his first full-size biplane in 1907, but could not complete tests until the end of that year. He had chosen the Brooklands race-track for his experiments and had to wait until the racing season finished before commencing serious trials. The 6hp J.A.P. engine used in the first trials was not sufficiently powerful to get Roe airborne. He therefore resorted to borrowing a 24hp Antoinette engine from the French manufacturer, Levasseur. With this, and after much modification to the wings and airscrews, he was able to

Alliott Verdon Roe (1877-1958).

A.V. Roe at the controls of his Triplane (1909) on Walthamstow marshes. Note that the aircraft is not covered in fabric.

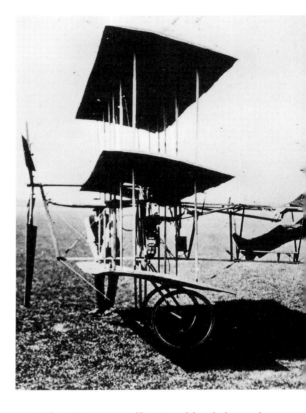

make a few successful hops. Financial pressures saw the return of the Levasseur engine to its maker and eviction from the Brooklands site.

In his search for a suitable testing ground, Roe's attention turned towards the Lea Valley where the Great Eastern Railway had established a new line in 1840. Roe was able to rent an arch, in 1909, underneath the brick viaduct on Walthamstow Marshes which took the railway spur across the River Lea to Chingford. The accommodation was ideally placed to allow rapid flight testing of aircraft after construction or modification.

It was from this particular site, on 13 July 1909, that A.V. Roe made his historic flight in a triplane, powered by a 9hp J.A.P. engine. This was not only an all-British first but a double first for the Lea Valley, as the engine was manufactured close by in the J.A.P. works at Tottenham, adding another chapter to the list of technological achievements for the region. A blue plaque, placed on the viaduct wall adjacent to the railway arch where the plane was housed and prepared, now marks the location of A.V. Roe's flight.

For a number of years there has been considerable confusion over claims concerning who made the first powered flight in Britain in an *all British* aircraft and the actual location where this occurred.

On 16 October 1908, almost five years after the Wright brothers, Wilbur and Orville, made their epic flight at Kitty Hawk, North Carolina, USA, S.F. Cody, an American, made the first official flight in Britain in British Army Aeroplane No.1. He covered a distance of 1,390 feet (423.7mtrs). J.T.C Moore-Brabazon, a Briton, flew 1,500 feet (457.2mtrs) in a French Voisin on 2 May 1909.

When Roe was still at Brooklands he took a biplane off the ground on 8 June 1908 achieving several hops of two to three feet above the race track. However, Roe did not make these early flights known until some two years later. The Gorrell Committee of the Royal Aero Club, in 1928-1929, disallowed A.V. Roe's claim to having been the first to fly in Britain on the grounds that he had not flown for a sufficient distance. They ruled that Moore-Brabazon was the first genuine Briton in the French aircraft.

Nevertheless, it was A.V. Roe's flight from Walthamstow Marshes on 13 July 1909, when he flew about 100 feet (30.5mtrs) in his triplane, that was the first official flight of an *all British aircraft with a British pilot*. On 23 July 1909, Roe extended the flight distance to 900 feet (274.3mtrs) at an average height of 10 feet (3.04mtrs).

An Avro Lancaster (c.1943) of the famous 617 ('Dambusters') Squadron which has been adapted to carry the Barnes Wallace bouncing bomb. The explosive for the bomb (RDX) was developed at part of the Royal Gunpowder Mills complex at Waltham Abbey, Essex.

Early in 1912, although this time not in the Lea Valley, Roe claimed a further success, when his company built and flew the first enclosed aeroplane in the world.

We in the modern world owe a great debt of gratitude to the vision, determination and resourcefulness of these early pioneers. Imagine how slow technical progress would have been if these visionaries had not been able to secure the necessary finances to turn their dreams into reality.

REFERENCES

'An Air Pioneer in Walthamstow', Occasional Publication no.15 (Walthamstow Antiquarian Society)

Jackson, A.J., *Avro Aircraft Since 1908* (Putnam Aeronautical Books, 1965, revised and updated by R.T. Jackson, 1990)

Who Was Who, 1851-1960

Tottenham's 'Stamp' of Approval

IF PEOPLE living or working in Tottenham were to be asked what the area's claim to fame is, odds on the reply will be 'the Tottenham Hotspur Football Club'. If the follow-up question is 'Have you heard of Rowland Hill?', the retort might be, 'what position does he play?'.

In 1827 Rowland Hill (later Sir) purchased Bruce Castle, now the local history museum in the London Borough of Haringey. In the 16th century the building was the Tottenham Manor House, the name being taken from Robert Bruce's father, the Lord of the Manor. Wings were added to the building in the 18th century which have given it its now familiar shape. Interestingly, the road outside Bruce Castle is named Lordship Lane, hinting at the building's former importance.

Hill's plan when purchasing Bruce Castle was to turn it into a boarding school. This he did with his younger brother Arthur, who acted with him as joint Headmaster. The new school was to be run along similar lines to a school Rowland had established earlier with his brother Matthew close to Birmingham.

For the early 19th century the brothers' education methods were highly radical. Corporal punishment, a commonly used weapon in the education armoury of the day, did not feature in the Hills' methods of discipline. Instead, responsibility was encouraged in a rather revolutionary and democratic way through teaching pupils the art of self-government and self-education. It would appear that the brothers had inherited some of their ideas from their father, Thomas Wright Hill, who had established a school at Hill Top near Birmingham, after becoming disenchanted with his business activities. Thomas Hill, with his radical beliefs, encouraged his sons to engage in scientific experiments. This form of education was to play an important part in Rowland's later life.

By the late 1820s, Rowland Hill's health began to suffer from his self-imposed workload and it became clear that he would have to give up teaching. Leaving Arthur to run the school, Hill put his earlier scientific education to use by designing a rotary printing press. It was hoped that the machine's design would be able to take advantage of a new paper production technology developed in France. The French technique, which was revolutionary for the day, produced paper in large rolls rather than in single sheets. Hill probably thought his invention would allow a reduction of Stamp Duty, effectively a tax, which had been levied by the Government.

At the time it was customary to impress a penny stamp onto each individual sheet of newspaper. This operation was carried out by the Stamp Office prior to printing. By printing on a continuous roll and cutting the paper afterwards,

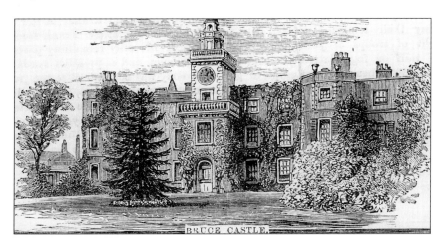

Engraving of Bruce Castle, c.1870.

Hill may have cleverly reasoned that the amount of duty could be reduced.

However, the Government Stamp Office were in no mood to lose revenue and would not allow the stamp to be impressed into the paper as the roll moved through the machine. Hill was therefore forced to shelve his invention. Had his scheme been accepted then his proposed method for printing newspapers would have been considerably ahead of the mechanised printing presses which did not arrive until some thirty years later.

Hill appears to have been an extraordinarily multi-talented person, seemingly able to turn his hand to almost anything. In 1833 he was part of an association which was formed to colonise South Australia and two years later he was appointed secretary to the South Australia Commission. It would seem that during this period Hill had begun to explore ways to bring down the cost of postage. For some time he had been aware that it was too expensive for poor people to communicate with friends and relatives over long distances. At the time postal charges were calculated by distance and each enclosure was charged as a separate letter. The cost of a letter travelling from London to Edinburgh, for example, was 1s. 4½d.—an excessive charge by early 19th-century standards.

By 1835 Hill had observed that large revenue surpluses had been raised through the postal charge levy. However, he had also noticed that the amount of mail handled by the post office over the previous 20 years had not increased in line with the growth in population, as one might expect, but had actually fallen. This, Hill reasoned, was due to the illicit carriage of mail brought about by the high postal charges.

The discovery galvanised Hill into actively campaigning, mainly through pamphlets, for a reduction in postal charges. Questions were raised on how this might be achieved without serious loss of revenue to government. It became clear to Hill that he would have to gain a greater understanding of how the post office functioned.

Sir Rowland Hill, K.C.B. (1795-1879), originator of the penny postage system.

He first tried to gain access to the London post office to examine their methods of working, but this initiative was obstructed. Hill pursued his quest outside the post office and discovered other ways of obtaining the information he required.

When Hill eventually appeared before a commission of post office inquiry on 13 February 1837, he had already carried out a considerable amount of research into the operation of the postal service. This he had done through a long and tedious study, *inter alia*, of official government reports. Equipped with a better understanding of how postal charges were levied, he could confidently put forward his case.

Hill proposed to the commission that a standard postage charge be set and the revenue collected by means of 'a bit of paper just large enough to bear the stamp, and covered at the back with a glutinous wash'. The idea was probably not original and seems to have been taken from a proposal by Charles Knight, made

Engraving of a Royal Mail delivery pony and trap, c.1879.

over two years earlier. Knight was a newspaper editor and also Hill's publisher. At the time, Knight had suggested that stamped wrappers could be used when sending newspapers by post, showing that postage had been pre-paid. In those days, it was customary for the recipient to pay the postal charges. Apart from being an inefficient way of gathering revenue, it was particularly unfair to the receiver of unsolicited correspondence.

It was not until 10 January 1840, after much parliamentary debate and considerable toing and froing, that the penny post was finally established in Britain. Perhaps when next we complain of dry lips and tongue at the annual Christmas lick, a thought could be spared for Rowland Hill and Charles Knight's simple idea which revolutionised world-wide communication by making postal charges affordable.

REFERENCES

Hill, Rowland and [his nephew] Hill, George Birkbeck, *The Life of Sir Rowland Hill and the History of the Penny Black* (De La Rue & Co., 1880)

Pegram, Jean, 'From Manor House to Museum', Bulletin no.28 (Hornsey Historical Society)

Lee, Sidney (ed.), *Dictionary of National Biography* (Smith Elder & Co., 1909)

Engraving of an early Royal Mail delivery van, c.1879.

21

So What's Famous About Hackney?

WHEN RESEARCHING into the industrial history of the Lea Valley, the author can easily recognise the London boroughs of Enfield, Haringey, Newham, Tower Hamlets and Waltham Forest as the source of a host of epoch-making firsts for the region. In the 19th century, some of the largest iron-clad warships in the world were built at the Thames Ironworks, on the Essex bank (now Newham) of the River Lea at Leamouth, where the waters of the Valley enter the great river of the metropolis.

The birthplace of the post-industrial revolution, the 'Technological Revolution', can be identified at Ponders End in Enfield at the beginning of the 20th century. Here the electronic age began with the invention of the world's first diode valve, patented by Professor Ambrose Fleming in 1904 and developed at the laboratory of Ediswan at Ponders End.

Across the River Lea from the northern end of Hackney, on Walthamstow Marsh, A.V. Roe made the first powered flight in an all-British triplane in 1909.

In 1936, Hackney's neighbour (now Haringey) saw yet another historic event when the British Broadcasting Corporation began the world's first public service high definition television transmissions from its studios in Alexandra Palace, Wood Green. Earlier in the century (1903), Harris Lebus claimed to have built the world's largest furniture factory beside the River Lea at Tottenham.

In the 19th century William Henry Perkin, while living in what is now Tower Hamlets, discovered the world's first synthetic dye—mauvine.

So what was Hackney's claim to fame? Scanning the borough's records, the industrial history seems pretty ordinary. During the late 18th and 19th centuries the principal industries were brick making, crepe manufacture, calico printing, cloth bleaching and dyeing, paint and varnish making, piano making, and clothes, footware and furniture manufacture. However, in 1862, an early form of plastic, said to be the first

example of its kind in Britain, was patented by Alexander Parks who called the material 'Parkesine'.

While perhaps not strictly an industrial first, Hackney can claim the world's largest 19th-century hothouse. In the early 1740s, Johann Busch (anglicised to John Busch or John Bush) came to Hackney from Germany and became a supplier of unusual plants to several botanical gardens and in particular to those of Princess Augusta (daughter-in-law of George II). Her plant collection eventually formed the basis of the Royal Botanic Gardens, Kew. In 1771 Busch was invited to Russia and commissioned, by Catherine the Great, to lay out gardens in the 'English-style'.

Following in Busch's footsteps in the early 1760s was another German, Joachim Conrad Loddiges, a gardener who settled in Hackney. He was first employed by Dr. (later Sir) John Baptist Silvester to landscape the grounds of his house near what is now Mare Street. Later Loddiges opened a nursery in the area and specialised in importing rare seeds and plants from around the world. Many of these were cultivated and re-exported in special packaging which he designed.

The desire to grow plants which were accustomed to warm and humid conditions in Britain's unfriendly climate caused Loddiges to experiment with what was then leading-edge technology. Loddiges built a number of hot-houses which were heated by stoves. The largest of these reached a height of 40ft. and measured 80ft. in length by 40ft. in width. This structure was to become known as the Grand Palm House and from there plants were supplied to decorate the Great Exhibition of 1851 at the Crystal Palace which had been built in Hyde Park, London.

Later, the exhibition's designer, Sir Joseph Paxton, again bought a number of plants from Loddiges Nursery to adorn the Crystal Palace when it moved to its new home at Sydenham (the current site of the BBC's television transmitter mast). Among the plants purchased

Joachim Conrad Loddiges
(1738-1826).

Palms inside the Crystal Palace at the Great Exhibition
of 1851, probably supplied by Loddiges of Hackney.

A Giant Mauritius Fan
Palm on its way, pulled by
thirty-two horses, to the
re-erected Crystal Palace
at Sydenham in south
London c.1854.

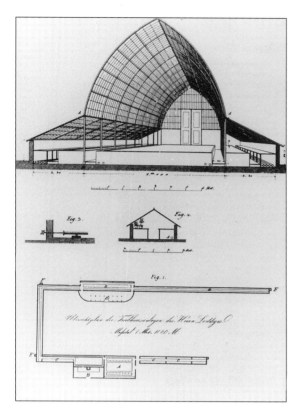

*A drawing of Loddiges
Grand Palm House.*

was an enormous Mauritius fan palm weighing some 15 tons, which in 1854 was transported from Hackney to Sydenham on a special carriage pulled by 32 horses. Soon after this, Loddiges' lease expired and the nursery closed in the mid-1850s. Anyone who visits the Mare Street area of Hackney today will no doubt require superhuman powers to imagine Loddiges' successful botanical business.

Like many east London boroughs, Hackney's heritage owes much, and can be historically traced, to those who came from abroad and settled in the region. The knowledge and expertise brought by the many immigrant groups to the Lea Valley community has helped to influence and enrich our lives to this present day. Passing down their legacy of skills through successive generations has helped to enhance the standard of living we enjoy today. We can express our gratitude to those early pioneers by sharing our acquired knowledge with others, thereby ensuring that the benefits which we have derived are carried forward into the 21st century.

REFERENCES

Currie, C.R.J. (ed.), *The Victoria History of the County of Middlesex*, vol.10: Hackney Parish (University of London Institute of Historical Research, Oxford University Press, 1995)

Lewis, Jim, 'So What's Famous About Hackney?', *Business in Hackney*, issue 9 (October 1996)

Solman, David , *Loddiges of Hackney* (Hackney Society, 1995)

22

A 19th-century Gift to the 20th century

IT IS HARD to imagine our lives today without plastic. The material, in various guises, packages our food, surrounds our televisions, computers and audio equipment, and is used extensively by the building industry in plumbing and wiring. Plastic also replaces many other traditional materials which are essential in the construction and finishing of our homes, from waterproof membranes to thermal insulation and protection from the elements. This highly versatile material has also given engineers and scientists the capability to design and develop various artificial body parts which have helped sustain and improve the quality of life.

Over the years there has been much debate about the true inventor of plastic. As with other claims in the history of discovery there is nearly always someone, other than the publicly recognised inventor, who has played an important part in the development process, but lacks recognition. For example Marconi, as we have been led to believe through a plethora of articles and history books, was the inventor of wireless. But without the earlier work of Faraday, Hertz, Lodge and others, Marconi would not have had a product to invent.

Nevertheless, what Marconi did was to exploit the available embryonic technology and develop a system which required a commercially viable product to promote it. In his particular case it was the wireless transmitter and receiver. The invention, or rather the development, of plastic has several similarities with Marconi's work on wireless.

Depending on which encyclopedia the reader chooses to consult, it will be discovered that the materials which can be initially identified as plastic were claimed by both America and Britain as an industrial first. In America, John W. Hyatt and Isaiah S. Hyatt developed Celluloid around 1868 and on 15 June in the following year they registered a United States patent (No.91,341) for the substance. However, in Britain, Alexander Parkes had developed a material from a solution of gun-cotton and ether, which after further

Alexander Parkes (1813-1890), discoverer of an early form of plastic.

refinement he called Parkesine which he patented in 1855 (No.2359).

In May 1862, what was to become the Royal Society of Arts organised a great International Exhibition in Kensington, London. Here, Alexander Parkes and his brother Henry, a qualified chemist some 11 years his junior, exhibited a range of brown coloured Parkesine products in a rather small sample show-case. An information leaflet handed out at the time explained that the material could be used for making 'tubes, buttons, combs, knife-handles, pens, pen-holders etc'. Also it was stated that the material could be made as 'hard as ivory, transparent or opaque and could be worked in dies and pressure or used as a coating'. This is probably the first time a plastic material and a summary of its uses had been placed before the public.

Visiting the Exhibition was a Daniel Spill who managed a factory owned by his brother George in Wallis Road, Hackney Wick in east London. At the time Spill's factory was engaged in the manufacture of waterproof cloth. It would seem that the business was successful for it is recorded that capes and groundsheets were supplied to the troops during the Crimean War (1853-1855).

Spill had become interested in a claim made by Parkes that the material, Parkesine, was waterproof, and wrote inviting him to a meeting at his Hackney Wick factory. Parkes, for some

The Xylonite factory at Highams Park, London at the turn of the century. A low level industrial estate now stands on the site.

unknown reason, did not reply to Spill nor take up the offer until nine months later. When Parkes eventually came to Hackney Wick, in 1864, the meeting resulted in an agreement drawn up and signed by the two men to manufacture Parkesine in Spill's factory. This was to be done by utilising some of Spill's rubber processing machinery.

Over the next 18 months, Daniel Spill and George Loeber, a rubber mill operator, spent all their time (with much help from Parkes) experimenting and endeavouring to perfect the material so that a commercially viable quantity could be produced. In June 1866, with the support of investors such as Henry Bessemer, the steelmaker, the Parkesine Company was formed with a capital of £100,000. The Hackney Wick factory was expanded in anticipation of the rewards from the new business.

However, by 1868, due to mounting disagreement between Parkes and Spill over a range of issues, the Company was wound up. Daniel Spill appears to have been an extremely determined man with faith in the new material, as on 10 May 1869 he registered the Xylonite Company Limited, the name Xylonite being derived from the Greek word meaning wood. This, presumably, like wood, has something to do with the versatility of the material in its many uses.

Spill took on the lease of additional premises at 122 Homerton High Street, Hackney and erected new buildings in nearby MacIntosh Lane. By the end of 1869 Spill had made 16 tonnes of the new material mainly in the form of white sheets. These were used to produce knife-handles and an early insulator for the rapidly expanding telegraph industry which was beginning to use miles of electric cable.

Unfortunately these early successes were not indicators of instant prosperity and by 1872 the Xylonite Company had gone into liquidation.

Nevertheless, Spill, in his usual determined manner, carried on trading under his own name and by 1875 he appears to have moved his business to 124 Homerton High Street. About this time, Levi Parsons Merriam, who had tried to introduce the American equivalent of Xylonite (Celluloid) into Britain, moved into Spill's vacated premises at number 122. In 1877 Spill and Merriam had formed, separately, the British Xylonite Company and the Homerton Manufacturing Company. These two businesses were merged in 1879 and in 1884 Merriam took control of the joint company. Before the merger, Merriam had acquired the Impermeable Collar and Cuff Company of Bower Road, Hackney Wick.

With Merriam in control, sheet production was moved to Suffolk in 1887 and in 1896 the British Xylonite Company bought Jack's Farm at Hale End, Walthamstow, in east London to build a new factory. In 1897 the Homerton site was sold and finished product manufacture was moved to the new site at Hale End, continuing the link with the Lea Valley and plastic.

After a number of changes and amalgamations the more familiar name of Halex Limited was born in the late 1930s. By 1960 the factory saw further expansion with the opening of a new production facility on the Hale End site. However, the expansion of the plant was short-lived as by spring 1971 the factory had closed and the buildings were eventually demolished,

Employees outside the Xylonite Homerton factory in 1897. By the smart dress it would appear that they were posing for a photographer, perhaps on some special occasion, rather than attending work.

Lighting and covers for THORN EMI Lighting.

Parts for business information systems

Silver cabinet for Ferguson TX 10" portable colour TV.

Modern plastic mouldings of items which are part of our every day life.

thereby breaking the long tradition of discovery, experimentation and development of plastic and its associated products in the Lea Valley.

Unfortunately there are no remaining clues to enable the interested visitor to guess the site's historic connections. Currently the site, in Larkshall Road, which is close to Highams Park railway station on the Liverpool Street to Chingford line, is occupied by low-level warehousing and a DIY store.

REFERENCES

Britannica Micropedia Ready Reference, vol.3 (Chicago, 1992)

Collins Encyclopedia, vol.5 (New York, 1996)

Currie, C.R.J. (ed.), *The Victoria History of London* (Institute of Historical Research); *The Victoria History of the County of Middlesex*, vol.10: Hackney Parish (Oxford University Press, 1973)

Karwatka, Dennis, *Technology's Past*, (Prakken Publications, Inc., Kentucky, 1996)

Merriam, John, *Pioneering in Plastics—the Story of Xylonite* (East Anglia Magazine Ltd., Ipswich, 1976)

The Oxford English Dictionary, vol.11 (Clarendon Press, Oxford, 1989)

Powell, W.R. (ed.), *The Victoria History of the Counties of England: A History of Essex*, vol.6 (Oxford University Press, 1973)

23

The Aesthetic Side of Industrial Stratford

THOSE OF AN AGE to remember Stratford in the 1950s and 1960s will no doubt recall an area engulfed by unpleasant smells which emanated from the profusion of chemical processing, paint and animal product rendering industries. Many of these industries had been forced to relocate from London's Middlesex side of the River Lea to the Essex side in the 19th century under an Act of Parliament, introduced, *inter alia*, to improve the health of the City.

Thomas Frye (1710-1762), founder of the Bow Porcelain Factory.

A range of Bow blue and white wares. The saucer c.1748-50, in the middle, is contrasted with the two plates on either side from the 1760s.

Today, although there is a considerable amount of redevelopment taking place at Stratford, there are also large pockets of decay which are a legacy of the industries which once concentrated in the area. Given the picture of a grimy industrial landscape, it is hard to imagine that things of beauty were once created there which sold internationally and received artistic acclaim. Even today, these objects are much valued and sought after by collectors.

It was in the 18th century that the initiative to manufacture beautiful objects came to Stratford—brought by a man from across the Irish sea. Thomas Frye was born in Dublin in 1710 and as a young man he studied to become a painter and engraver. Frye came to England in 1732 and it would appear that he became proficient in his chosen profession as in 1738 he was commissioned by the Saddlers' Company of London to paint a full length portrait of H.R.H. Frederick, Prince of Wales.

In 1744 Frye founded the Bow China Works with George Arnold, who was a wealthy merchant and an Alderman of Cheap Ward in the City of London and Master of the Haberdashers'

Company (in 1735), and Edward Heylin, a merchant of Bow. The works were located on land and buildings on a site west of the River Lea which Arnold and Heylin had jointly purchased and with Frye they established the Bow China Works. In the same year year Frye and Heylin took out the first British patent for 'A method of manufacturing a certain material whereby a ware might be made of the same nature or kind, and equal to, if not exceeding in goodness and beauty, China and Porcelain ware imported from abroad'. The process was based on an imported material (probably kaolin or china clay) from America named 'Unaker' by the Cherokee.

After much experimentation by Frye with additives, such as phosphate of lime recovered from animal bones, he obtained a second patent in November 1749, this time solely in his own

A late view, c.1835, of the much modified, 12th-century first Bow Bridge over the River Lea shortly before its demolition. The picture gives a general impression of how the area may have looked at the time of the Bow Porcelain Factory which was located approximately 250 metres east of the bridge.

name. In this patent Frye claimed that he was able to make 'a certain ware which is not inferior in beauty and fineness and is rather superior in strength than the earthenware that is brought from the East Indies and is commonly known by the name of China, Japan or porcelain ware'. What Frye had developed, through experiment, was what is now more commonly known as 'bone-china'.

All the ingredients required to make porcelain were available to Frye in Britain, although it is not clear if he ever switched from his American supplier. Some researchers have speculated that because shipments of 'Unaker'

were cheaper from America than could be obtained locally, its use allowed Frye to undercut considerably other manufacturers in the production of household table-wares. On this basis it is suggested that Frye continued to use the material. On the other hand, it has been argued that 'the almost complete loss of contemporary accounts of the English porcelain manufactories, of their methods of business and of their financial account books, adequately explains our present ignorance of contemporary comment on the American source of Bow's china-clay'. Clearly we are unable to say with complete confidence that, during any phase of

A photograph of the second Bow Bridge, taken in 1893, carrying the main road over the River Lea.

manufacture, Frye never sourced his materials from anywhere other than America.

By 1749 it is recorded that the Bow China Works was operating under the name of Alderman Arnold & Co., in the parish of West Ham, Stratford, the factory now being situated on the east side of the River Lea (west of Marshgate Lane on the north side of Stratford High Street). The factory was at first called 'New Canton' as it was said to have been modelled on the lines of the porcelain factories in the Chinese city.

By September 1750, after the death of George Arnold in June that year, the factory had become Frye & Company, although sometime after 1752 it would seem that Messrs. Weatherby and Crowther were the proprietors. However, Hugh Tait, in a paper read in 1962, has expressed doubt that Crowther was ever a proprietor of the Bow China Works at Stratford and his evidence for this is quite convincing.

It would appear that Weatherby & Crowther were sales agents for Bow porcelain, with a warehouse at St Catherine, near the Tower, and a retail outlet in Cornhill. Weatherby died in 1762 and his partner Crowther was declared bankrupt in 1763, his warehouse stock being sold at auction the following year. Tait has therefore reasoned that, as the Bow China Works at Stratford was not involved in the bankruptcy and

continued as a business until at least 1775, Crowther and his partner were probably never in complete control of the company.

Frye left the company in 1759 due to poor health and retired to Wales, although he is reported to have returned to London at a later date to paint miniature portraits. He died in 1762. The manufacture of porcelain at Bow reached its zenith under Frye in 1758 when the factory employed some 300 people, 90 of whom were skilled painters, many coming from Staffordshire, the centre of the pottery industry. In 1776 the whole factory, complete with models and moulds, was sold to William Duesbury who transferred production to his Derby works. This marked the end of porcelain production at the Bow China Works in the Lea Valley, the first place in Britain where successful manufacture of the material occurred on a commercial scale.

REFERENCES

Bernard, W., *The American Side, English Blue & White* (Faber & Faber, 1963)

Powell, W.R. (ed.), *West Ham 1886-1986* (Council of the London Borough of Newham, 1986)

Solon, M.L., *A Brief History of Old English Porcelain* (Bemrose & Sons Ltd., 1903)

Tait, Hugh, 'The Bow Factory under Alderman Arnold and Thomas Frye (1747-1759)', a paper read at the Rembrandt Hotel (Mr. and Mrs. J.A. Wilby), on 8 February 1962

4 The Man With His Head in the Clouds

LISTEN to a radio, open a newspaper or switch on a television and at some time the listener, reader or viewer will be sure to encounter information about the weather. We are preoccupied with such questions as whether it will rain, whether it will be sunny or cloudy, but seldom do we give a thought to those early pioneers who studied the elements. However, the patient observations and recording of the seasons, particularly by one man, have led to descriptions that have become international standards in the recognition of cloud formations and patterns.

Luke Howard was born into a Quaker family in London in November 1772. After an education at a Quaker school at Burford in Oxfordshire, Howard, at the age of 15, was apprenticed for seven years to Ollive Sims, a pharmaceutical chemist in Stockport. On returning to London he set up on his own account as a chemist in Fleet Street. After only a short time in business he became a partner of William Allen, a chemical manufacturer who had premises at Plough Court, Lombard Street. Soon, Howard was running the company's manufacturing laboratories at Plaistow, at the time a small village in east London. There, in 1796, he married Mariabella Eliot and set up home in Chesterton House, Balaam Street.

During Howard's apprenticeship in Stockport, it would appear that he had become interested in botany. This would account for the subject of his first scientific paper, 'A microscopic investigation into the species of Pollen', read before the Linnean Society in March 1800.

In 1801 Howard began a register of meteorological readings 'as a daily record of the Phoenomena [sic], regarded as passing occurences [sic] … [and] as a continued notation of facts interesting to the Philosopher, and from which he may deduce results, for the purpose of extending our knowledge of the Oeconomy of the seasons'.

Howard put his meteorological observations from his home and those gathered from walks in Plaistow to good use when, in 1804, he read a paper before the Askesian Society entitled, 'The Modification of Clouds'. Here he discussed not only the nature and height of clouds but he also gave detailed descriptions to their formations giving them names such as Cirrus, Cumulus, Stratus, Cirro-Cumulus, Cirro-Stratus, Cumulo-Stratus and Cumulo-Cirro-Stratus vel Nimbus. Essentially, much of Howard's terminology is used internationally in the description of weather patterns, even to this day, which is why he is generally regarded as the father of modern meteorology.

In 1807 the partnership with William Allen was dissolved and Howard continued to develop the manufacturing side of the business which had moved to Stratford. However, his interest and enthusiasm for observing the weather remained, even after he had moved to Tottenham

Luke Howard (1772-1864), the founder of modern meteorology.

John Constable's (1776-1821) Study of Clouds at Hampstead, *painted at Hampstead, London between 10-11am on 11 September 1821. Constable was said to have been influenced in his work by Howard.*

in 1812, where he still kept a detailed meteorological record. The results of Howard's observations between 1806 and 1830 were published in three volumes entitled *The Climate of London* which was considered by many to be his most important work.

Howard, when living in Tottenham, had acquired a small estate at Ackworth in Yorkshire which he was able to use to further his observations into the behaviour of the weather. With the aid of an elderly Barograph Clock, designed by Alexander Cumming (1733-1814) who was a mathematician, mechanic and watchmaker, Howard was able to chart and record in detail the barometric pressures in London between 1807 and 1823, which he compared with later readings taken at Ackworth between 1824 and 1841. The information gleaned helped him to compile his theory of the 18-year cycle in British weather. Howard published his theory in 1842, within one year of completing his research. The speed of publication had been brought about because Howard believed that his findings, on the cyclic nature of the climate, would be of particular benefit to those in agriculture. Much of the recorded data, including barograph charts, was published in Howard's *Barometrographia*.

Howard, who was elected a Fellow of the Royal Society in 1821, was a prolific writer. Apart from publishing many learned papers and articles on his beloved subject, he contributed considerably to Rees's *Cyclopaedia* and between 1833 and 1837 he edited *The Yorkshireman*, a religious and literary journal.

After several years of failing health, Howard died at Tottenham on 21 March 1864. His eternal legacy to us all is a greater appreciation of the clouds and their composition. Luke Howard's writing on clouds even stimulated the great painter John Constable, who has recorded pictorially the beauty which Howard spent his life observing.

REFERENCES

Author unknown, *Luke Howard—Father of Modern Meteorology, 1772-1864* (Science Museum pamphlet, 1972)

Blench, Brian J.R., 'Luke Howard and his Contribution to Meteorology', *Weather*, vol.18, no.3 (March 1963)

Powell, W.R. (ed.), *West Ham 1886-1986* (Council of the London Borough of Newham, 1986)

Royal Society Proceedings, 1865

Stephen, Leslie & Lee, Sidney (eds.), *Dictionary of National Biography* (Smith Elder & Co., 1908)

The Man with the Imaginative Flare

WHILE QUITE A LOT has been written about the Royal Gunpowder Mills at Waltham Abbey, the Royal Small Arms Factory at Enfield Lock, and to a lesser extent, the London Armoury Company at Bow, there has been relatively little published regarding William Congreve's Rocket Factory next to Bromley-by-Bow, on the Essex side of the River Lea. In fact, trying to trace the origins of the factory through the various local and national archive sources has proved to be a formidable task. However it is known, from the *Victoria County History of Essex*, that a rocket factory existed on West Ham marshes, currently the site of a redundant gasworks, at least between the years 1840 and 1862, a considerable time after Congreve's invention of the gunpowder rocket in 1804.

By good fortune the author was able to examine the 'Survey of the parish of West Ham in the county of Essex', taken by a James Clayton in 1821, where it can be established that Sir William Congreve 'occupied' four plots of land on the West Ham marshes which were 'owned' by Sir Robert Wigram. Plot numbers 199, 201 and 204 are referred to as 'marsh pasture', while plot 203 is listed as 'rocket manufactory and premises'. Here we have clear evidence that Congreve was yet another of those now famous names who had chosen the Lea Valley region to establish their innovative industries.

William Congreve, the eldest son of the similarly named Sir William Congreve, was born on 20 May 1772. His father held the rank of Lieutenant-General, Colonel Commandant of the Royal Artillery, also holding the powerful positions of Comptroller of the Royal Laboratory at Woolwich and Superintendent of Military Machines. After an education at the Royal Academy at Woolwich, young Congreve was attached to the Royal Laboratory at Woolwich in 1791, where his father still held the position of Comptroller of the establishment. It is perhaps little wonder that, after such an upbringing, the son was to develop a considerable interest in military matters, weaponry and machinery.

Congreve had become aware that the rockets used by the military in India had only a short range, usually not exceeding 1,000 yards. He was also aware of General Desagulier's experiments, some years earlier, with large rockets, but few of these had risen from their stands. Around 1804, it occurred to Congreve that '… the projectile force of the rocket is exerted without any reaction upon the point from which it is discharged'. This gave him the idea that a rocket, as a weapon of war, might be launched from a boat. His reasoning had led him to believe that a rocket, launched as a projectile in this manner, would be more acceptable than that of a ball when shot from a cannon which always resulted in the weapon's violent recoil.

Congreve manufactured a number of gunpowder rockets in London (obtaining the propellant from the Royal Gunpowder Mills at

'Survey of the parish of West Ham in the county of Essex', taken by James Clayton in 1821. Plots 199, 201, 203 and 204 are registered in the name of Sir William Congreave [sic]. Note that plot 203 is described as a 'Rocket Manufactory and premes'.

198	Ditto	Matthews	Marsh pasture	5	1	35
199	Ditto	Sir W. Congreave	ditto	4	3	30
200	Ditto	Huntindon	Osiers	1	3	0
201	Ditto	Sir W. Congreave	Marsh pasture	5	0	17
202	Ditto	Matthews	ditto	10	2	2
203	Ditto	Sir W. Congreave	Rocket Manufactory and premes	0	1	25
204	Ditto	Ditto	Marsh pasture	5	2	25
205	Carter	Maxwell	ditto	16	1	27

Waltham Abbey) but he found their range disappointing, not travelling more than five to six hundred yards. However, he persevered with his experiments and eventually he was able to increase the range to over 1,500 yards without dramatically altering the characteristic of the projectile. As his

Major-General Sir William Congreve, Bt., M.P., F.R.S. (1772-1828).

experiments were becoming more costly he approached Lord Chatham, elder brother of the Prime Minister and at the time Master General of Ordnance, for permission to have some larger rockets made at Woolwich. Again, after experimentation, Congreve was faced with disappointment as his newly manufactured rockets could only travel about six hundred yards. However, he doggedly continued to experiment and eventually he was able to achieve a range of around 2,000 yards.

With the confidence of his experiments behind him, Congreve approached William Pitt (the younger), then Prime Minister, with a plan '... for the annoyance of Boulonge [*sic*] by fire rockets'. At the time Britain was engaged in the struggle with Napoleon and any plan which might have frustrated the French would no doubt have gained the sympathetic ear of Government. After trials at Woolwich, which were attended by Pitt, Lord Castlereagh and Lord Mulgrave, it was agreed that an attack should be mounted on the French flotilla. The plan was to fire a large quantity of rockets from the launches of the English men-of-war belonging to the Boulogne squadron which had been placed under the command of Rear-Admiral Sir Sidney Smith.

Ten launches were suitably equipped to carry out the attack which was planned for the night of 21 November 1805. At 8pm that evening, after a

day of calm, the wind shifted to the north west, reaching gale force, and the attack had to be abandoned. In 1806 Congreve again approached the Board of Ordnance and suggested that another attempt be made to attack Boulogne. The rockets which Congreve now proposed to use against the French had reached a later stage in their development, having been constructed with iron cases; his earlier versions had cases made of paper.

Eventually an attack was unleashed on Boulogne by some 200 rockets launched from 18 boats which had been rowed from their mother ships and positioned in the bay. Within ten minutes, so it has been reported, the town was on fire. However, the control of the missiles' accuracy in this particular experiment has been called into question, as it has been written that a

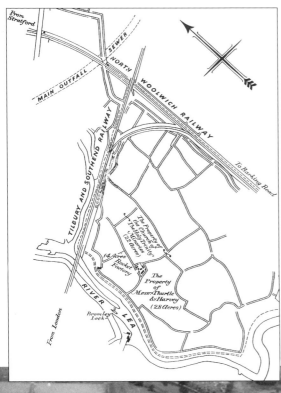

few of the rockets went off course, veering to the left and damaging some of the French flotilla lying at anchor in the harbour. While this may have been an unexpected bonus for the British, it does illustrate how unpredictable this new weapon could be.

Congreve rockets were used in a number of battles during the Napoleonic War, from Copenhagen in 1807 to Waterloo in 1815. The missile was also used against Fort McHenry in the 18-month conflict (June 1812 to December

Left. A map of the Bromley-by-Bow area prior to 1870, before the gasworks were built, showing William Congreve's Rocket Factory adjacent to the River Lea.

Below. Redundant Grade II listed gasholders at the Bromley-by-Bow gasworks close to the site where Sir William Congreve's Rocket Factory once stood.

1814) with America and the occasion has been commemorated in the United States' national anthem by the wording 'the rockets' red glare'.

There can be little doubt that Congreve, apart from being enthusiastic for the rocket as a new weapon of war, pioneered and developed battlefield ideas for his missiles which have become commonplace today, for example, the parachute flare. In what Congreve calls his 'light ball' or 'floating carcass' rocket, he explains that the

> Rocket, containing in its head, a parachute with a light ball or carcass attached to it by a slight chain. This Rocket being fired nearly perpendicularly into the air, the head is burst off at its greatest altitude, by a very small explosion, which, though it ignites the light ball, does not injure the parachute; but by liberating it from the Rocket, leaves it suspended in the air, in which situation, as a light ball, it will continue to give a very brilliant light, illuminating the atmosphere for nearly ten minutes; or as a carcass, in a tolerable breeze, will float in the air, and convey the fire for several miles, unperceived and unconsumed, if only the match of the carcass be ignited and the disengagement of the parachute.

However, one can conclude from research at the Public Record Office, Kew and elsewhere that the rocket, like many other early forms of experimental device, was not an instant or complete success. The rocket acted more as a psychological weapon which often provoked fear in the enemy. Soldiers, on the receiving end, were unaccustomed to the missile's noise and glare and they were probably less concerned with its accuracy and destructive power. A letter from a Lieutenant Lindsey (21 November 1810), on active service in Spain, makes the point that while the odd rocket used in the bombardment of a town would set a house on fire, he complained that in general '… others could not be seen to produce any effect'.

It is clear that the Congreve rocket lacked accuracy and was subject to the mercy of the wind. An incident during the Peninsular War illustrates just how temperamental the rocket could be. As a quantity of rockets had been shipped to Spain for use by the British army, the Duke of Wellington wished to witness a demonstration of their effectiveness under battle conditions. It was therefore arranged that the army would fire a number of rockets at the enemy who were positioned some distance away on the other side of a hill. Unfortunately the flight of the rockets was across the prevailing wind and, after firing, some returned hissing and spluttering amongst the ranks of British troops. It was said that after the experience Wellington 'entertained a dislike of rockets from that day forward'. Although it is probably fair to conclude that the Congreve rocket was not the complete success the inventor had wished for, it does show that he was an early innovator in this field of warfare.

REFERENCES
Public Record Office, Kew: WO1/1120; WO1/1123
Author unknown, *Explosives—OHMS Bicentenary*, booklet to commemorate 200 years (1787-1987) of Government ownership of the Royal Gunpowder Mills (Waltham Abbey)
Congreve, William, *The Details of the Rocket System* (London, 1814)
Page, William (ed.), *The Victoria History of the Counties of England—History of the County of Essex*, vol.2 (Archibald Constable & Co., Ltd., 1907)
West Ham Local History Archive, London
Clayton, James, *A Survey of the Parish of West Ham in the County of Essex* (Ingatestone, 1821)
Dance, F.J., *A Survey of Industry—West Ham—up to 1920* (London, 1970)
Parker, W.A., 'The Development of the Heavy Chemical Industry of West Ham', unpublished MSc thesis (London, 1950)

Note: In 1814 William Congreve succeeded his father as second Baronet and as Comptroller of the Royal Laboratory. The following year he introduced a number of improvements to the Royal Gunpowder Mills at Waltham Abbey and in particular an improved type of granulating machine which he patented (No.3937). It has been recorded that the operation of the machine could not be bettered during the years that gunpowder production lasted.

The Man Who 'Dyed' Young

WHILE STRICTLY not a Lea Valley man, it would seem disrespectful to omit any reference, within this book, to William Henry Perkin (later Sir), chemist, born 12 March 1838, at Shadwell in London's east end. To ignore Perkin, a close neighbour of the Lea Valley, would be to lose the opportunity of a vital clue to understanding how one part of the region's diverse industrial base developed. Perkin's work not only influenced and encouraged the early chemical and cloth dyeing industries within the region, but his discoveries were responsible for the revolution which took place in the manufacture and production of perfumes and life-saving drugs throughout the world.

Shadwell is now part of the London Borough of Tower Hamlets whose eastern borders touch the west bank of the River Lea, the river being about two miles, as the crow flies, from Perkin's birthplace at 3 King David Lane, where his father, George Fowler Perkin, had set up home and from where he ran his local building and carpentry business.

Perkin was a talented child with many and varied interests. He had shown practical engineering skills at an early age by making wooden models and had even attempted to build a steam engine. Perkin had an artistic side, too, maintaining a love for drawing and painting throughout his life and it was also said that he inherited a 'pronounced musical talent' from his father. However, it is for his work as a chemist that he became best known, his youthful imagination being fired by a friend who had shown him some simple experiments in the growing of crystals.

After a private education at a local school, Perkin, in 1851, entered the City of London School where he had the good fortune to receive twice-weekly lectures on chemistry and natural philosophy from Thomas Hall, a former student and graduate of the Royal College of Chemistry. Hall had spotted young Perkin's enthusiasm for the subject and allowed the lad to prepare some of the experiments for his lectures, even letting

A charcoal portrait of William Henry Perkin at the age of twenty-eight.

him assist on occasions.

When it was announced that the eminent scientist and discoverer of benzene, Michael Faraday, was to give a series of lectures on electricity at the Royal Institution, Hall, it is believed, encouraged Perkin to write for permission to attend. This the young man did and received an invitation from Faraday himself. Little did Perkin realise at the time that in 1861, almost 10 years hence, he himself would be delivering a lecture before the Chemical Society 'On Colouring Matters Derived from Coal Tar', which Faraday would attend.

By the age of 15 it would seem that Perkin had soaked up all he could at the City of London School and, with Hall's support, he was encouraged to try for a place at the Royal College of Chemistry in Oxford Street, London. This was a relatively new institute which had merged with the School of Mines. The College, in 1845, had been fortunate in securing the services of a talented German chemist, August Wilhelm Hofmann as director, a man renowned for his inspiring lectures and commitment to leading-edge research.

However, Perkin's father was at first opposed to the idea of his son following the profession of a chemist, as he had wanted him to become an architect. Hall was instrumental in persuading Perkin senior that his son's talents lay elsewhere and the lad was eventually allowed to enrol at the Royal College of Chemistry. There Perkin, and another young student, Arthur Church (later

Professor), had shown such early promise that Hofmann assigned them to his private laboratory to carry out research. The two students, who were given adjacent work benches, soon realised that they shared similar interests and became firm friends. Both found their enthusiasm for chemistry so great that they set up laboratories in their own homes to pursue their research interests outside college.

It was during the Easter holiday of 1856, in the makeshift laboratory at his father's house, then at King David's Fort, Shadwell, a little distance from his birthplace, that Perkin was to make a discovery that would revolutionise the world that we live in today. While trying to find an artificial substitute for quinine, by heating a mixture of aniline sulphate and potassium dichromate, Perkin accidentally discovered the world's first synthetic dye: mauveine.

Instead of throwing away the results of his failed quinine experiment, he added alcohol to the rather nasty looking precipitate at the bottom of his filter paper and observed that it took on an attractive purple colour. It is at this stage that the modern-day observer can marvel at the pure genius and incredible foresight of this young man, well beyond his years. For Perkin was only 17; an age when many of today's young people would be studying for their A level examinations. Under such circumstances, it might be asked what had caused the spark of inspiration in Perkin's brain which had allowed him to overcome what appeared to be a failed experiment. It must have taken a great leap of imagination for him to realise that what he had on his hands, metaphorically speaking, was a recipe for a major commercial success.

Perkin confided his discovery to his friend, Arthur Church, who, probably because his family were lawyers, saw the need to advise the young man to seek immediate patent protection. Then, through an acquaintance, Perkin was introduced to the dyeing firm of J. Pullar & Son, at Perth, in Scotland. Perkin visited the company and left samples for them to examine. John Pullar, after completing his tests, was initially cautious of Perkin's discovery, but he saw the superiority of the new dyestuff over what was currently available.

At the time, purple was a popular colour with wealthy people and was said to be a

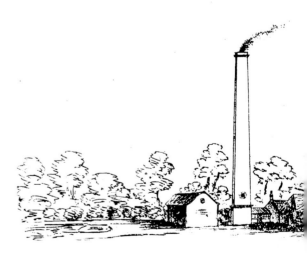

favourite of Queen Victoria. Unfortunately clothing so coloured tended to fade rapidly, which was probably why it was popular with the rich, as only they could afford to buy new clothes regularly when theirs began to lack lustre.

Through Pullar, an introduction was made to Thomas Keith, who had a silk dyeing business in Bethnal Green, not far from Perkin's home. Like Pullar, Keith carried out his own tests, also showing cautious enthusiasm for the new discovery. This, it would appear, was all the encouragement Perkin needed and he decided to set up a factory to manufacture his discovery on a large scale. Perkin resigned his research post

Top right. A Portrait of Sir William Henry Perkin (1838-1907) holding what appears to be a skein of wool which has been dyed mauve.

Right. A drawing of the first apparatus used in the manufacture of nitrobenzene by W.H. Perkin. The cast-iron container is fitted with two tubes and a stirring handle can be seen along with a door and fastening mechanism. One tube was used to introduce benzene and sulphuric acid and the other to let nitrous fumes escape.

Below right. W.H. Perkin's later apparatus for manufacturing nitrobenzene. Here a series of cast iron containers can be observed and a system of line shafting can be seen which was used to operate the stirring mechanism.

A sketch of Perkin's Greenford Green, Middlesex factory c.1858.

with Hofmann and, with the help of his elder brother, Thomas Dix Perkin, and his father, a factory was built on a green-field site north-west of the capital, near a branch of the Regent Canal at Greenford, Middlesex.

At first one wonders why Perkin chose to place his factory so far away from his east end of London roots. There he could have obtained a plentiful supply of coal-tar products, essential for his manufacturing processes. From the 1830s there were at least three gasworks in the vicinity, at Brick Lane, Curtain Road and Shoreditch.

However, from the early part of the 19th century various Acts of Parliament had been passed which tried to prohibit industry and the community from discharging chemical and other waste into the rivers of the capital. These noxious effluents often found their way into the River Thames, from where the private water companies took their supplies for the city. This clearly posed, and became, a major risk to public health.

In 1856, the year before Perkin commenced building his new factory at Greenford, the Metropolitan Board of Works was set up under an Act of Parliament. This body was the first attempt to bring about a system of local self-government. It divided the capital into 39 districts. With all the pressures to clean-up and improve the health of the capital, it is conceivable that Perkin did not wish to waste time in wading through the bureaucratic morass to set up in business locally—better to move outside the metropolis where the rules were different.

While the Lea Valley did not gain Perkin as a major manufacturer, the world at large was introduced to the dawn of a whole new chemical era which would, in the future, see the development of plastics, petrol additives, carbon fibres, synthetic rubber and much more. Sir William Henry Perkin died on 14 July 1907 and it is fair to say that this man alone was responsible for founding the coal-tar dyestuffs industry which provided the catalyst for a whole new generation of research chemists to revolutionise chemical technology. The results of Perkin's work and the contribution, particularly of those who followed, has brought us many of the creature comforts we take for granted and enjoy today.

REFERENCES

Author unknown, *Born to the Purple—Sir William Henry Perkin and the Origin of Organic Chemistry* (an I.C.I. publication, Manchester)

Author unknown, *Perkin Centenary London—100 Years of Synthetic Dyestuffs* (Pergamon Press, 1958)

Bazalgette, William Joseph, 'On the Main Drainage of London and the Interception of the Sewage from the River Thames', *Minutes of Proceedings of the Institution of Civil Engineers*, 14 March 1865, vol.24 (1864-1865)

Bazalgette, William Joseph, 'Address of Sir J.W. Bazalgette, President', *Minutes of Proceedings of the Institution of Civil Engineers*, 8 January 1884

Cory, W.G., *East London Industries* (Longman Green & Co., 1876)

Everard, Stirling, *The History of the Gas Light & Coke Company 1812-1949* (A. & C. Black, 1949)

James, Mary, *The History of Chemistry in Essex and East London* (The Essex Section Trust of the Royal Society of Chemistry, 1992)

Leaback, D.H., *Perkin in the East End of London* (Authentica Publications, 1991)

Leaback, D.H., 'Discovery in the East-End—A Personal Account of Discovery Against a Seemingly Very Ordinary East-End Background', *East London Record*, no.12 (East London History Society, 1989)

Lee, Sidney (ed.), *Dictionary of National Biography*, second supplement, vol.3 (Smith Elder & Co., 1912)

Morris, Laurence E., 'The Perkin Centenary', *Textile Printer, Bleacher and Finisher*, vol.cxv, no.10 (11 May 1956)

27

The Man Who Did London's Dirty Work

JOSEPH WILLIAM BAZALGETTE (later Sir Joseph)—not to be confused with his father, Joseph William Bazalgette, a Commander in the Royal Navy—was born in Enfield, Middlesex, on 28 March 1819. The precise place of his birth at Enfield is not known.

After an education at private schools, Bazalgette became a pupil of Sir John Benjamin MacNeill in 1836, the same year in which he joined the Institution of Civil Engineers. MacNeill had begun his career under the famous civil engineer Thomas Telford and became one of his deputies. Telford clearly had a high regard for MacNeill as, after his death in 1834, it was discovered that he had remembered him in his will.

Bazalgette's early experience of carrying out work on a drainage and reclamation project in the north of Ireland, and his involvement in other tasks as a pupil of MacNeill, helped to shape what was to become a highly distinguished career in civil engineering. By 1842 he had set up at Westminster as a consulting engineer, mainly engaged on railway work.

In 1849 Bazalgette became a member of The Metropolitan Commission of Sewers. Appointments to this body were Government nominations. The new organisation had been set up in the previous year to replace the eight district bodies who had been responsible for the drainage of London. Previously, little thought had been given to a method of uniform drainage for the capital and as a consequence the system was extremely inefficient. Because there had not been one coordinating body charged with design and development, there were considerable differences of size, shape and fall of the sewers at the district boundaries: larger sewers discharged into smaller ones and egg-shaped sewers with narrow parts uppermost were coupled to similar sewers built in reverse.

Until 1815 it was illegal to discharge sewage or other noxious material into the sewers as it had been deemed they should only be used to carry surface water. At the time, cesspools were

Sir Joseph Bazalgette (1819-1891).

considered to be the only place appropriate for depositing household sewage. However, with London's increasing population cesspools were unable to cope with the waste and the law was either deliberately relaxed, or perhaps a blind eye was turned by the authorities. It was not until 1847 that an Act was passed which made it compulsory to drain household waste into London's sewers. Within six years 30,000 cesspools had been abolished as the effluent was directed into a modified, but not redesigned, sewerage system. Now surface water and raw sewage combined to be discharged directly into the River Thames. In many instances the outflows of sewage were close to where the private water companies took their supplies.

Between 1848 and 1855 the Metropolitan Commission of Sewers had been reconstituted six times with successive new appointments. This made it almost impossible for the body to implement any worthwhile schemes of sufficient magnitude to alleviate the growing problem of a highly polluted Thames. The water companies which took their supplies from the Thames came under increasing pressure as public concern for health intensified. In London, deaths from cholera alone, in 1854, amounted to almost twenty thousand. Although Bazalgette was appointed Chief Engineer of the fifth and sixth Commissions, his early plans for solving London's drainage problems were frustrated.

In 1856, under an Act of Parliament, the Metropolitan Board of Works was set up. This body was the first attempt to bring about a system of local self-government by dividing the capital into 39 districts. The City of London and the largest parishes, like Lambeth and Marylebone, formed separate districts, while the smaller parishes were amalgamated into further districts of manageable size. Bazalgette was appointed Chief Engineer to this new body and instructed to prepare plans for the drainage of London. This he duly did and the scheme was approved by the Board. However, Her Majesty's First Commissioner of Works had the power of veto and Bazalgette's plan was delayed. After much complicated negotiation and discussion, his recommendations were eventually adopted and work began on the scheme in 1859.

It is possible that Members of Parliament may have put pressure on those delaying progress, as, in summer 1858 when temperatures in the metropolis exceeded 90 degrees Fahrenheit, the stench from the polluted Thames became unbearable. Conditions became so bad that the windows of the Houses of Parliament had to be covered with curtains soaked in chloride of lime to try to overcome the dreadful smell. The episode became known as the 'Great Stink'.

Bazalgette's grand plan was to construct a sewerage system which, as far as possible, would rely upon gravity and surface water to ensure that the effluent was kept flowing. He also planned to divert the waste away from outlets which fed directly into the Thames near the centre of London, to a place some 14 miles below

The Abbey Mills Pumping Station, Stratford, London, built in c.1868. Because of its ornate design, the building became known as the 'Cathedral of Sewage'. Originally beam engines were employed to lift the lower level sewage into the Northern Outfall sewer (constructed between 1860 and 1865) where the effluent mixed with surface water before being discharge into the River Thames at Barking. Later improvements to the system saw the separation of solids from the effluent which were taken out to sea in 'gravy boats' for dumping.

London Bridge. He had calculated that by discharging at this distance there would be little chance of the sewage being brought back to the metropolis by the turning tide.

As Bazalgette had discovered, it was not possible, for reasons already outlined, to use the existing sewerage network. He therefore arranged for new sewers to be constructed which consisted of 1,300 miles of brick-built tunnels. On the north and south sides of the Thames, separate outfall sewers were built at a higher level so that they could carry the effluent to the discharge points further down the river. To raise the sludge from the lower level gravity sewers which were between thirty and forty feet below the new outfall sewers, pumps were used. On the south side the Southern Outfall Sewer was serviced by the pumping station at Crossness, while the Northern Outfall Sewer was fed by the

A drawing showing a section of the overflow chamber at the junction of the northern, high and middle level sewers.

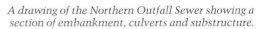

A drawing of the Northern Outfall Sewer showing a section of embankment, culverts and substructure.

Abbey Mills pumping station, situated on the Essex side of the River Lea.

Presumably, in an effort to disguise the unromantic occupation of the Abbey Mills pumping station from the local residents, the building was constructed on a grand scale. In its creation several different coloured bricks were used, the effect being so flamboyant that the building was nicknamed the 'Cathedral of Sewage'. The design was the work of Bazalgette and Edmund Cooper, the building being shaped in the form of a crucifix. Each of the four sections housed twin coal-fired beam engines and the exhaust from these was carried away by two highly ornate Moorish style chimneys. Although the Abbey Mills pumping station still stands, the two chimneys were demolished during the Second World War, leaving only the stone bases. It was thought that they acted as landmarks for the enemy, allowing the bombers to pin-point targets when attacking the London Docks.

Before his death in March 1891 Bazalgette would have been rightly entitled to look back on his remarkable career with pride. He had restored, with an army of workmen, craftsmen and skilled engineers, the health of London's population.

REFERENCES

Bazalgette, William Joseph, 'On the Main Drainage of London and the Interception of the Sewage from the River Thames', *Minutes of Proceedings of the Institution of Civil Engineers*, 14 March 1865, vol.24 (1864-1865)

Bazalgette, William Joseph, 'Address of Sir J.W. Bazalgette, President', *Minutes of Proceedings of the Institution of Civil Engineers*, 8 January 1884, vol.24

Lee, Sidney (ed.), *Dictionary of National Biography*, vol.XXII (Smith Elder & Co., 1909)

Note: It would make a good research project to discover the actual address at Enfield where William Joseph Bazalgette was born.

28

The Man Who Wanted to Copy

DAVID GESTETNER was born in Csorna, Hungary in 1854. His first experience of work, for a short time, was that of a stockbroker's clerk at the Vienna Stock Exchange. After the collapse of the financial market in Vienna, the young Gestetner moved to America in 1875 to seek his fortune. However, things did not go according to plan and for a time he was forced to support himself meagrely by selling Japanese children's kites on the streets of Chicago. It was while engaged in this enterprise that Gestetner noticed the special qualities of the paper from which his kites were made. The paper, a type of tissue, was comprised of long fibres, essentially non-porous, which gave the material lightness and strength. A wax coating made the paper waterproof.

It is not exactly clear when, or for how long, Gestetner had harboured thoughts of making copies of documents. However, there is little doubt that his observations of the paper, from which the Japanese kite's were made, had given him the inspiration to make the world's first practical stencil.

The Neo-cyclostyle Duplicating Apparatus, patent No.11832, 1888. Printed on the label which is on the outside of the box is a caution: each genuine sheet of Neo-cyclostyle paper must bear the signature of the inventor—D Gestetner.

After coming to Britain in 1881, on 16 August that year, Gestetner registered Patent No.11,832, 'Improvements in "Cyclostyle" pens for producing stencils to be employed in the reproduction of writings, drawings and other delineations'. Gestetner's invention was practical, yet exceedingly simple. The Cyclostyle pen, as he termed it, had at its tip a small toothed wheel which revolved when the user wrote in the normal way. The stencil itself was constructed from the special Japanese paper, called Takamatsu, which Gestetner had discovered earlier when selling kites. When the paper was placed on a hard smooth surface, and written on with a Cyclostyle pen, the toothed wheel perforated the exterior wax and exposed the fibres beneath. This action produced, or cut, the stencil. When ink was applied by a roller to the impervious wax surface of the paper, it could only pass through the neatly cut perforations to the sheet of copy paper below.

Under high magnification the perforations cut by the Cyclostyle wheel look irregular, but when viewed by the naked eye the line appears continuous. For its day the invention proved to be a considerable commercial success. Unfortunately, like most advances in technology, it had its human downside, in this case making the work, although tedious, of many copying clerks redundant.

In America, there was a challenge to the uniqueness of Gestetner's British patent from a company with an interest in Thomas Edison's 'Electric Pen', which was a development of the telegraph system, where morse signals were recorded by punching holes in paper with a sharp pointed reciprocating needle. A.B. Dick, in April 1889, brought an action in the U.S. Circuit Court claiming that the Cyclostyle was an infringement of Edison's patent. However, after listening to and weighing up the evidence, Judge Coxe ruled in favour of the Cyclostyle, a decision which indicated that Gestetner's invention was in fact unique. The ruling, along with the commercial success of the Cyclostyle pen,

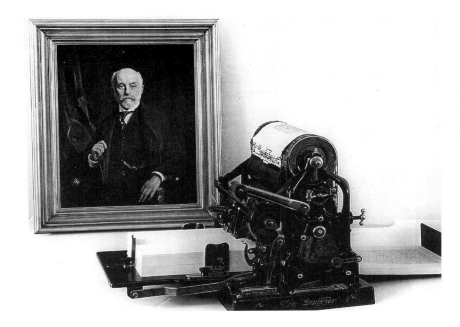

The 1924 Gestetner duplicator—note how open the mechanism is. In the background is a portrait of the founder of the Company, David Gestetner (1854-1939).

supported the claim that the instrument could reproduce handwriting more smoothly than any other comparable product of the day.

The early business of David Gestetner, the 'Cyclostyle Company', began its existence in London's East End, operating from small premises in Sun Street, Shoreditch. With a young woman assistant Gestetner started manufacturing Cyclostyle pens, wax stencils and duplicating ink which he advertised and marketed as a kit. In 1888, presumably from experience gained from the marketplace, Gestetner made a slight modification to the pen by setting the toothed wheel at an angle to the shaft. This improved the instrument's manoeuvrability which further enhanced its commercial success. The instrument and the process was re-named the 'Neo-cyclostyle Duplicating Apparatus'.

Gestetner's decision to re-brand and modify the product can be seen as a significant move in the fortunes of the company, which launched it and its founder on the road to international success, putting the name of Gestetner before the world. Although the technology of the stencil appears simple with the benefit of 20th-century hindsight, one must acknowledge the determination of these early pioneers who

worked very much with trial-and-error experimentation. Of the stencil, it has often been said that there were two secrets in the art of duplicating: the paper and the pen.

By the late 19th century typewriters were becoming increasingly popular in the office and this embryonic technology can be likened to the growth of personal computers today. However, the introduction of this machine posed a new set of duplicating difficulties. Gestetner quickly realised that, if these problems could be overcome, there would be considerable financial rewards for his company.

The first real obstacle was that the type face on the individual typewriter keys could not perforate the paper which he had developed for his stencils. With much experimentation the solution was found once again in Japan, with a new type of paper called Yoshino. This had an open-textured and porous structure, as opposed to the closer meshed fibre of the earlier stencil. However, there were yet more difficulties to be overcome.

The type face cut into the new paper which could leave it weakened and full of holes. For example, letters composed of a continuous line like O, Q and D, posed particular problems. The difficulty was partially overcome by introducing

A view, looking north, showing part of the front of the Gestetner factory and offices in Broad Lane, Tottenham, London c.1949.

another sheet of paper, known as muslin tissue, in front of the wax stencil. This had the effect of reducing the impact from the type hammers. To improve the accuracy of the final duplicated image, the typist had to place a thin piece of board between the stencil and the typewriter platten to make a hard surface for the type hammer to strike against.

From the late 19th century until at least the 1950s, the Gestetner company perfected the manufacture of the stencil by incorporating new materials as they became commercially available and by developing new production techniques. This resulted in a range of special stencils which could be produced on a printing press. The company also produced stencils which were sensitive to light (designed for photocopying or camera work) and 'electronic stencils' made by spark discharge.

In parallel with the early refinement of the stencil, Gestetner began to work on increasing the speed of duplication and by 1900 he had patented a twin-cylinder rotary machine with the stencil mounted on a silk screen. The model was manufactured in quantity and marketed in 1902. This heralded what was to be the start, at least for Gestetner, of a continuing revolution in the design of the duplicator. Improvements to the

mechanism followed with the introduction of an automatic paper feed system and by 1909 the first electrically powered machine was born.

The premises at Sun Street had become too small for the growing company and in 1906 a new factory was acquired in Broad Lane, Tottenham. Over the years, with demand increasing and the expansion of international trade, Gestetner was to become the largest duplicator manufacturer in the world. This saw not only the considerable expansion of the Broad Lane plant, which retained duplicator manufacturing, but the opening of new facilities in Tottenham and elsewhere. These ranged from other types of manufacturing, distribution and training located in Tottenham, to the production of photocopying machines at Byfleet, Surrey, offset litho machines at Wellingborough, Northamptonshire and the setting up of new factories for producing and coating paper at Kilbagie and Stirling in Scotland.

Gestetner had grown from a two-person operation in the 1880s with a rather crude product to a multi-national company with a substantial product range. By the late 1970s there were some 10,000 people working outside Britain, mainly engaged in marketing, sales and service, while manufacturing was still carried

Artists impression of the Gestetner factory at Broad Lane, Tottenham, London c.1955.

out in the UK, although the acquisition of the Rex-Rotary company slightly altered this dominance.

By the early 1980s, with the increasing popularity of office photocopying equipment over the ink duplicator, there was growing concern locally that Gestetner's Tottenham plant was now making an outdated product. Unfortunately it would seem that local concerns were justified as the Broad Lane plant was soon to close. Nevertheless, it should not be forgotten that David Gestetner, whose name is now synonymous with business machinery, brought to the Lea Valley a simple piece of technology which revolutionised the office world and provided research, development and manufacturing jobs for the local and a much wider community.

REFERENCES

Author unknown, *Cyclostyle—the Little Wheel That Started a Big Revolution* (a Gestetner publication)

Author unknown, 'Tottenham's Future Jobs—Who Decides?' (report published by Tottenham Employment Group, 1979)

Currie, C.R.J. (ed.), *The Victoria History of the County of Middlesex* (University of London Institute of Historical Research, Oxford University Press, 1995)

Proudfoot, W.B., *The Origin of Stencil Duplicating* (Hutchinson, 1972)

29

Harris Lebus – the Maker of Affordable Furniture

IN THE 1840s, Louis Lebus, one of the earliest Jewish immigrant furniture workers to have come to Britain, arrived in Hull from Breslau in Germany. By 1857 he had set up a workshop to pursue his craft in Whitechapel, in London's East End. His business must have been relatively successful as in 1875 he moved to larger premises in Stepney.

After Louis's death in 1879 the business was taken over by his 27-year-old son Harris who in 1885 moved the firm yet again to a multi-storey building in Tabernacle Street. This was closer to Curtain Road in the district of Shoreditch where many of the East End's furniture and associated industries were concentrated.

An interesting fact was brought to the attention of the author by William Massil, a former manufacturer of turned wooden parts for the industry. He explained that in the early 19th century the mainly small craft workshops which made up the furniture trade were divided between two distinct areas of London. There were those businesses in the West End, which were referred to as the 'honourable' side, while those in the East End were known as the 'dishonourable' side. Massil suggests that it was the West-End manufacturers who supplied the prestigious London retailers until the middle of the 19th century, but then it became the turn of the East-End furniture trade to take over as the main suppliers. According to Massil, the perceived notion that the West End produced the best quality furniture while the East End manufactured the cheap is totally erroneous. There were, he remarked, considerable variations in quality within both sectors of the industry.

The progress of Harris Lebus was slightly delayed in 1894 by a serious fire. After rebuilding, the firm became the largest furniture manufacturer in Britain, employing in excess of one thousand workers by the end of the century. By 1900, further manufacturing expansion to meet long-term consumer demand for furniture was out of the question in the cramped streets of the East End. Therefore, the decision was taken to build a new factory on a 13½-acre green-field site by the River Lea at Tottenham. Subsequently more land was purchased, increasing the area of the site to 40 acres. The East-End premises in Tabernacle Street were not abandoned but converted to showrooms to display Lebus products.

Many other East-End furniture firms, looking to expand, followed the example of Lebus and

A Lebus advertisement from the trade journal The Cabinet Maker, *19 July 1947, which claimed that the Finsbury Works at Tottenham was the largest furniture factory in the world.*

Harris Lebus

Off-loading timber from a River Lea barge into the Lebus storage and drying sheds in Ferry Lane, Tottenham, London c.1950.

established themselves on other sites in the upper Lea Valley where land was relatively cheap. There they discovered how useful the river was, as timber could be brought by barge directly from the London Docks and stored in warehouses beside the waterway where it could dry until required for manufacture.

The new Lebus factory was completed by 1904. However the majority of the workforce had to commute by public transport from the East End. This arrangement proved unsatisfactory for many, so Lebus encouraged the building of houses nearby which promoted the growth of south Tottenham.

By the start of the Second World War the factory employed almost 8,000 people, later claiming in its advertising literature to be the largest furniture manufacturer in the world. During the hostilities of 1939 to 1945 the furniture industry played a major part in the war effort by manufacturing sections of aeroplanes and other essential equipment for the Allied Forces.

Many of the workers, as well as the owners, in the furniture industry were Jewish immigrants who had left Europe to avoid persecution. They

had arrived in Britain with little more than the skills they possessed. It was perhaps somewhat ironic that these skills, and those passed down from the earlier immigrants, would become a vital asset in the struggle against Nazism when several of the Lea Valley furniture factories were taken over by the British Government for war work.

Harris Lebus would no doubt have been justly proud to have seen the expansion of the furniture industry out of the East End to sites in the upper Lea Valley where it grew and flourished. Sadly his premature death in 1907 at the age of 55 did not allow this.

By 1969 Lebus had left Tottenham, signalling the decline of the Lea Valley furniture industry. The Lebus site was eventually acquired by the Greater London Council who were responsible for the demolition of the factory on the southern part and the erection of a large housing estate on the cleared land.

A view from the air of the Harris Lebus factory, c.1950. In the foreground and to the left can be seen the vast area of storage and drying sheds which ran parallel to Ferry Lane, Tottenham. Two separate housing estates now stand on the site.

By the start of the 1980s the decline of the Lea Valley furniture industry had increased in momentum and it was clear that recovery was impossible. The decline had been brought about by a combination of events. These ranged from increasing pressure on the home industry from cheap imports, to the changing pattern of retail sales, which began to move away from traditional High Street furniture shops to the new superstores. Ironically, several of these new furniture warehouses have begun to occupy the space on industrial estates, where furniture factories once stood.

There are still remnants of the wood and furniture industry surviving in the Lea Valley today, although only a shadow of the former glory days of large-scale manufacturing. Also there are a modest number of craft-based workshops scattered throughout the region, carrying on the trade with skills handed down from early immigrants, a powerful reminder to us all of the magnificent contribution made to Britain by this resilient group of people.

REFERENCES

Interview with William I. Massil, London, 11/2/98

Massil, William I., *Immigrant Furniture Workers in London 1881-1939* (The Jewish Museum in association with the Geffrye Museum, London, 1997)

Sharman, Nick, 'Turning the Tables—Towards a Strategy for the London Furniture Industry' (Greater London Enterprise Board, 1985)

'Tottenham's Future Jobs, Who Decides?', Tottenham Employment Group (February 1979)

30

The London Movers and Shakers

WHEN WE THINK of the manufacture of road vehicles in this country our thoughts are usually drawn to the midland area of England and perhaps other regions such as the north west and north east. Here, particularly in the periods before and following the Second World War large quantities of commercial and domestic vehicles were produced, although in recent years there has been a rapid decline in the number of indigenous British manufacturers.

Latterly, due to new investment by overseas producers, with interests in increasing their share of the European market, there has been a revival of motor vehicle manufacturing in Britain. However, it is perhaps fair to say that seldom do we consider that London, and in particular the Lea Valley, was at one time a region which accommodated different generations of inventors and entrepreneurs who were responsible for much of the early development of road transport in Britain.

One of the earliest British engineers who had ideas of moving people en masse by road was Walter Hancock (1799-1852). Born at Marlborough, Wiltshire, Hancock served an apprenticeship to a London watchmaker and jeweller. It would appear, however, that Hancock had set his sights on heavier things for about 1824 he set up an engineering works in the east end of London, on the south side of Stratford High Street. Between 1824 and 1836, Hancock carried out experiments to demonstrate the practicality and the advantages of employing steam-carriages on common London roads.

In 1827 Hancock registered a patent for a coke-fired steam-engine which, due to its relatively small size and economic operation, made it eminently suitable for driving a range of road vehicles that he would soon develop.

The first steam-powered vehicle Hancock developed was a three wheeled, four seater car which was probably one of the first dedicated to moving people by road in Britain. In 1832 Hancock built another road vehicle, the 'Era', for the London and Brighton Steam Carriage

Walter Hancock (1799-1852).

The 'Enterprise', not the starship but a steam road coach, constructed in 1833 at Stratford in east London by Walter Hancock. This vehicle was capable of carrying 14 people.

A drawing of Walter Hancock's steam road coach 'ERA' built at Stratford in east London in 1834.

Company. Hancock's fame appears to have spread, as in April the following year, the London and Paddington Steam Carriage Company launched a service with his steam road coach, 'Enterprise', a vehicle which was capable of carrying fourteen passengers. By October 1833 another of Hancock's vehicles, the 'Autopsy', ran a limited service between London's Finsbury Square and Paddington and in October the following year he introduced the 'Erin' which ran between the City and Paddington.

There is no doubt that Hancock, for his day, was successful in advancing the technology of steam-powered road transport. One of his later projects was the 'Automaton', capable of carrying 22 passengers at a top speed of 20 miles per hour. However, it seems that the public had only taken a novelty interest in steam-powered road transport and, as a consequence, the companies who had invested in this new technology soon floundered through lack of revenue.

By the early 1840s Hancock had turned his energies to working with his brother Thomas who had premises in Goswell Road, London. At the time it is not clear if Walter appreciated the connection his move would make between his former experiments with road transport and the future discoveries of his brother.

Between 1820 and 1847, Thomas Hancock had taken out 16 patents relating to successful developments in the processing of India-rubber. His discoveries were of such significance that they were used by the now famous Charles Macintosh & Co., Manchester, in the preparation of waterproof garments. Hancock eventually became a partner in the firm although he still carried on with his business in London.

Perhaps even more importantly, Hancock was able to demonstrate that India-rubber, which became brittle when cold and sticky when hot, could be made stable against wide variations of temperature by the application of sulphur. On 21 November 1843 he patented a process based upon his discovery which was effectively an early form of vulcanising. Whether coincidence or not this discovery would seem to place both men on the road transport pioneering rostrum.

However, in America, Charles Goodyear, remembered for his association with vehicle tyres, had been working for a number of years on a similar method of vulcanising although he did not patent his process until 1844. Goodyear filed a legal suit against Hancock for allegedly stealing his idea, but he subsequently lost the case.

The next significant milestone in Lea Valley road transport began in a small workshop in the back garden of a house in Connaught Road, Walthamstow, East London. There between 1892-1894, Frederick Bremer (1872-1941) built the first British car to be powered by an internal combustion engine. In December 1894 the car had its first road trials in skeleton form, the body being added in January the following year.

There does not seem to have been any attempt to put the car into production; Bremer apparently built the vehicle by way of a personal challenge. After a period of virtual neglect in a garden shed, Bremer offered the car to Vestry House Museum, Walthamstow, where in 1931 it was placed on show. In 1962 the car was withdrawn from display so that restoration work could be carried out and in the autumn of the following year the vehicle's engine was coaxed into life.

The car was entered in the London to Brighton Veteran Car Run in November 1964 and broke down after completing 17 miles when the crankshaft failed. The following year it travelled the full 54 miles in 7 hours and 55 minutes, consuming three gallons of petrol, half a gallon of oil and 12 gallons of water. Frederick Bremer's car was returned to the Vestry House Museum where it remains on permanent display.

The next phase in the Lea Valley road transport story began with the unlikely intervention of Arthur Salisbury-Jones, a member of the Stock Exchange. Salisbury-Jones had hit on the idea of starting a large-scale motor-bus company to serve London's commuters, which, if successful, he would expand to cover the whole

of Britain. In January 1905 he launched the London Motor Omnibus Company which was so successful that other bus companies were quickly introduced to the metropolis. By the middle of 1907, Salisbury-Jones had over three hundred passenger-carrying vehicles on London's roads.

At the onset, Salisbury-Jones recognised that to achieve his aims and objectives he would need to control closely the manufacture and design of his vehicles. This he did by forming the Motor

Frederick Bremer (1872-1941).

Frederick Bremer, c.1893, and the car he built in his workshop behind his mother's house in Connaught Road, Walthamstow, London.

Omnibus Construction Company in February 1905 and in August the following year a small tin hut was rented in Hookers Lane, Walthamstow. Initially parts were purchased from a range of outside contractors to be assembled into vehicles. However, by January 1907 a new 30,000 square foot factory was opened at Hookers Lane which brought in-house much of the work provided previously by outside suppliers. By the following year the factory had doubled in size and the workforce had increased from the original six in 1906 to over five hundred and seventy.

An early A.E.C. 'B'-type bus, c.1914, of the London General Omnibus Company, built in Walthamstow. The bus ran on the 35 route from Leyton to the Elephant and Castle. Note the advertisements for Warner flats to rent, from 5s. 6d. to 10s. 6d. per week.

A view from the air of the A.E.C. factory which once stood at the junction of Blackhorse Lane and Forest Road, Walthamstow. The Company moved to Southall, Middlesex in c.1926.

ASSOCIATED EQUIPMENT Cº LTᴰ – WORKS & OFFICES
BUILDERS OF LONDON'S BUSES.
FROM THE AIR.

WALTHAMSTOW, LONDON, E.17.

standardisation and improvements in reliability and design which marked the creation and introduction of the now famous 'B'-type bus in October 1910.

Further structural changes took place in June 1912 when the vehicle construction side of the London General Omnibus Company was hived off to form the now more familiar Associated Equipment Company Limited (AEC). The restructuring had brought about improved efficiency and economies of scale which saw output of the 'B'-type increase from around three per week in October 1910 to 50 per week in March 1913. In this year, there were over 2,000 'B'-types on the road and their reliability was such that collectively, for every 100,000 miles travelled, there were only 14 unscheduled stops.

We all owe a great debt of gratitude to these early road transport pioneers, and in particular the vision and initiative of Arthur Salisbury-Jones, who laid the foundation of London Transport as we know it today.

The rapid expansion of the London transport system had caused vehicles to be purchased from a range of sources, many coming from overseas. Naturally the lack of standardisation caused a number of problems for the embryonic transport service, with vehicle safety and reliability featuring high on the list. In 1906 alone, it is recorded that London buses were involved in 2,448 accidents, many of them attributed to mechanical failure.

The rate of expansion had placed Salisbury-Jones and the other major bus operators in financial difficulties and it was clear that swift action needed to be taken or the whole operation would fail. It was therefore decided to restructure the companies through a merger and in 1908 the London General Omnibus Company was formed. This now provided the basis for vehicle

REFERENCES

Author unknown, *The Bremer Car—Its History & Technical Description* (London Borough of Waltham Forest Libraries & the Arts Department, *c.*1968)

Baldwin, Nick, 'AEC—The Early Years', *The Vintage Commercial Vehicle Magazine*, vol.3, no.9 (July/August 1987)

Day, John R., *The Story of the London Bus*, (L.T. Publication, 1973)

Dennis, John A., 'AEC—50 Years', *AEC Gazette* (November/December, 1962)

Karwatka, Dennis, *Technology's Past* (Prakken Publications Inc., Kentucky 1995)

Powell, W.R. (ed.), *The Victoria History of the Counties of England—A History of Essex*, vol.6 (Oxford University Press, 1973)

Thomson, L.A., *By Bus Coach and Tram in Walthamstow* (Walthamstow Antiquarian Society, 1971)

Townsin, Alan, 'The Way it Was at AEC', *The Vintage Commercial Vehicle Magazine*, vol.4, no.18 (January/February 1989)

The East End Engine Builders

STRATFORD in east London has witnessed the birth and development of a diverse range of industries from the making of artistic porcelain to the less attractive, and pungent, aroma of paint and chemical production. The establishment of the locomotive and carriage works of the Great Eastern Railway, that was based at Stratford also allowed generations of those—for whom there is something wondrous and beautiful about an engine that can run on rails belching smoke and steam while pulling a line of carriages or wagons—to indulge their hobby as train-spotters for over a century.

In 1848, the Eastern Counties Railway, as it was then known, moved its main locomotive workshops from Romford in Essex to a site in London's East End—located north-east of Stratford High Street. The Northern & Eastern Railway had already established a small repair shop at Stratford by 1839 and it was this facility which the Eastern Counties Railway leased in January 1844, perhaps with a view to the move in 1847-8. However, at the time, it is doubtful if the consolidation of the maintenance facility would be seen by those early planners as the start of a process which was to alter radically the social and economic face of Stratford for over a hundred years. From a site of about fifteen acres and a workforce of a few hundred around the middle of the 19th century, the facility had grown to 78 acres and employed over six thousand by the early part of the 20th century. By the 1920s the area occupied by the Great Eastern Railway, as it had become known in 1863, had almost doubled, to approximately 133 acres. This included the adjacent wagon building and repair facility at Temple Mills.

The move to Stratford not only brought the construction of new buildings, which would eventually lead to the carrying out of just about every type of rolling-stock repair imaginable, but also the building of 300 homes for the workforce and their families. Soon the district became known locally as 'Hudson's Town' after the railway entrepreneur, George Hudson. As late as

the 1950s the area was referred to as the 'New Town' by residents with long memories or those with railway connections. Even today, names like Waddington Road and Waddington Street (after Hudson's traffic manager) remind us of the area's railway heritage.

Over the years the railway works at Stratford were home to several notable engineers and superintendents who were responsible for the introduction of many new ideas and much technical innovation. In 1850, under John Viret Gooch, the works completed their first railway engine. This suggests a major change of direction for the Company, as it would have required a considerable amount of capital investment to complete such a venture. At the time, it must have been obvious to those responsible that once tooling-up for engine building had begun, there would be a need for ongoing investment in plant and machinery as the future technology of railway engines and other rolling-stock changed. Also, it will be remembered that the Stratford works was heavily committed to providing a maintenance and repair service for the Great Eastern Railway which, in the years to come, would no doubt become more complex as the amount of rolling-stock in circulation increased. However, the decision to build railway engines was successful, as construction lasted at Stratford up until the 1920s. During this period, 1,682 locomotives were built along with some 5,500 passenger vehicles and in excess of 33,000 goods wagons. This equates to a complete engine being turned out every two weeks over a period of 70 years—a remarkable achievement.

Other remarkable achievements occurred, particularly when Stratford was under the superintendence of James Holden, when the works responded to a number of engineering challenges. In February 1888 the Crewe works of the London North Western Railway had built a locomotive in 25½ hours. This record was quickly eclipsed in America by June the same year, at the Altoona works of the Pennsylvania Railway, when the time was lowered to 16½ hours. The challenge was taken up by the Stratford works when, in December 1891, the time for construction was brought down to 9 hours and 47 minutes—a world record for this class of engine. This record was never beaten.

The construction time included applying a single coat of protective grey paint to both engine and tender before the locomotive left the works for trials. In the case of the two previous records the engines had to be returned to their respective works for painting directly after completing their initial trials. The Stratford engine (0-6-0 small boilered freight type) was put into regular service hauling coal and had covered some 36,000 miles before being returned to the works for painting. Following 43 years of service she was scrapped in

January 1935 after covering the remarkable distance of 1,127,750 miles.

In the late 1880s the management of the Stratford works received complaints that they were polluting the River Lea, through a discharge of oil from the site. At the time the works operated an oil-gas plant to manufacture fuel for the lights in the company's carriages and it was the waste from this process which had leaked, or perhaps been deliberately discharged.

Holden addressed the problem and after a number of experiments he had an inspirational idea. His solution was to design a system which would burn the unwanted oil waste as a supplement to coal in the fireboxes of converted engines. The first of these conversions (2-4-0,

James Holden, in bowler hat, superintendent of the Great Eastern Railway Works, Stratford, east London, standing with crew and railway workers in front of an 0-4-4 engine, c.1897.

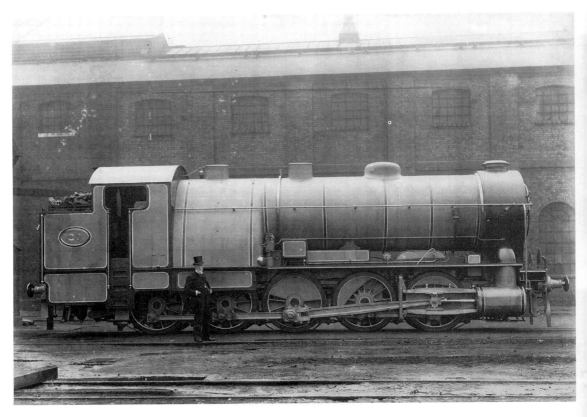

James Holden,
superintendent of the
Great Eastern Railway
Works, Stratford, east
London, standing in front
of the 'Decapod' (0-10-0)
railway engine, c.1902.
Although Holden was
responsible for the
engineering development
of this engine, much of
the 'Decapod's' design
was completed by the
talented railway engineer
Fred Russell.

The Drawing Office of the
Great Eastern Railway
Works, Stratford, east
London, c.1920.

Left. An engine under construction at the Great Eastern Railway Works, Stratford, east London.

Below left. The 'Decapod' under construction at the Great Eastern Railway Works, Stratford, east London.

Bottom left. A view of the general offices of the Great Eastern Railway Works, Stratford, east London, c.1920, after alterations had taken place. Note the design of the weather vane.

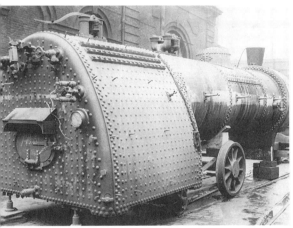

class T19), in 1893, carried 500 gallons of oil in a tank fitted to the tender. Later versions could carry 650 gallons. In all, around sixty such engines were converted to burn oil and it would appear that they did so until the supplies of the waste product ran out. It was then considered uneconomic to continue running these engines by bringing in alternative oil supplies.

By the turn of the century electric motive power was beginning to challenge steam as the new energy source. This gave designers the ability to build engines which could accelerate rapidly. Once again James Holden's engineering skills were put to the test to see if steam could remain competitive. His answer, in 1902, was to design the 'Decapod' (the first 0-10-0 in Britain) which could attain 30 m.p.h. in 30 seconds from a standing start pulling a train of 300 tons tare weight. Although, at the time, it was claimed that the 'Decapod' was the most powerful locomotive in the world, it was never put into regular service in its original form as the rate of acceleration was thought too severe for the bridges and track.

By January 1923 the Great Eastern Railway had merged with five other railway companies to form the London and North Eastern Railway and

The Robin Hood (4-6-0) being prepared at Stratford for an exhibition at Southend, Essex in 1956. After Nationalisation in 1948 the Works lost its Great Eastern Railway title and became British Railways.

it was shortly after this amalgamation that the decision was taken to cease building new rolling stock at Stratford. When the railways were nationalised in 1948 the Stratford works, now British Rail, continued its locomotive repair role. However, by the 1950s and 1960s new technology, in the form of electric and diesel locomotives, was being introduced as the railway networks pushed forward with programmes of modernisation. These measures were to have serious consequences for the Stratford works. Gradually departments closed and sections of the site were redeveloped to handle international freight transport. Nevertheless, a much reduced repair facility remained until 1991, when in March of that year the works finally closed, ending a proud chapter of London's East-End industrial history. The 151 years of railway engineering activity, between 1840 and 1991, are thought to represent a world record for continuous locomotive repair on one site.

REFERENCES

Aldrich, Langley C., *The Locomotives of the Great Eastern Railway—1862-1962* (C. Langley Aldrich, Essex, 1969)

Allen, Cecil J., *The Great Eastern Railway* (Ian Allan, 1976)

Author unknown, *Memoranda connected with the Locomotive and Carriage Works at Stratford and the Wagon Works at Temple Mills* (Great Eastern Railway, June 1921)

Farmer, Jack, *The Great Eastern Railway as I Knew it* (J.R. Farmer, Theydon Bois, 1990)

Hawkins, Chris & Reeve, George, *Great Eastern Railway, Part One—Stratford, Peterborough & Norwich Districts* (Wild Swan Publications Ltd., Oxford, 1986)

Gordon, W.J., *Our Home Railways—The Great Eastern Railway*, vol.1 (Frederick Warne & Co., 1910)

Pember, Geoffrey, *Great Eastern Railway 0-4-4 Tank Locomotives* (Great Eastern Railway Society, 1979)

Sainsbury, Frank, *West Ham 1886-1986* (Council of the London Borough of Newham, 1986)

32 The 'Art and Mystery' of the Floating Solid

ON A COLD MARCH day in the early 1840s with a keen east wind blowing along London's East India Road, a young George Corby Mackrow made his way from his home in Limehouse Fields to the works of Ditchburn and Mare. There, the lad was to discover if he would like to learn the 'Art and Mystery' of shipbuilding. The mystery being that he, as well as others of the day, expected a dry log of wood always to float when thrown into the water, but it was difficult to grasp the concept of how a ship made from iron did not sink.

Previously, the young Mackrow had tried coopering, silversmithing and optical instrument making, none of which were to his liking. However, Mackrow quickly found his vocation as a few weeks after his arrival he signed a seven-year apprenticeship agreement with the company. There is no doubt that the lad had chosen the right trade, as some years later he was to rise to the office of chief naval architect to the company, making him responsible for all technical aspects of marine design and construction. This promotion indicates that Mackrow had indeed solved the puzzle of the 'Art and Mystery'.

The shipyard of Ditchburn and Mare was on the Middlesex bank of the River Lea, close to where the waterway enters the River Thames, an area commonly known as Leamouth. On maps, this section of the river is referred to as Bow Creek. By the mid-1840s the yard was finding it difficult to obtain supplies of iron at competitive rates. Bringing in the material by rail would have been expensive, as the main line ran through Stratford, some distance from the yard. If Stratford had been used, it would have meant transferring iron to horse-drawn wagons for the final part of the journey. At the time the North Woolwich branch of the Eastern Counties and Thames Junction railway had not yet been completed.

To resolve the yard's difficulties Mare suggested to his partner that they should set up their own facility to roll iron plate. Clearly

Ditchburn was not sympathetic to the idea and the partnership dissolved. In 1846, the new firm of C.J. Mare & Co., was established on the opposite side of the River Lea in Essex. The move was to mark not only a significant milestone in the history of British shipbuilding, but that of the world.

Looking through the eyes of Mackrow, the young apprentice, we learn that Mare was a particularly single-minded man prepared to face considerable odds to see his convictions through. It has been suggested that Mare's new venture was considered decidedly foolhardy by many. One of Mackrow's early jobs was to mark, with wooden stakes, the site for two slips where ship and boatbuilding could commence. Apparently Mackrow and his fellow workmates nicknamed the site 'Frog Island' and we are told that the rushes which grew there on the swampy ground came up to his waist. During the period of the spring tides much of the site became submerged. Nevertheless, Mare was initially successful in laying down eight boats for the Citizen Company, which was one of two sizeable operators plying their trade on the Thames.

The outbreak of the Crimean War in 1853 saw an increase in both wood and iron shipbuilding. Mare's yard not only received orders from the British Admiralty but also from the French Government. It is recorded that the yard built four wooden despatch vessels, four gunboats, two large despatch boats and some 12 iron mortar boats. Two floating batteries were also constructed for the French Government, comprising a wooden shell plated with 3½ inches (9cm) of armour. These were to be used for attacking the fortified coastal positions at the Crimea.

By 1856 Mare was in financial difficulty and the running of the company was taken over by his father-in-law, Peter Rolt, who assumed control as Chairman. The company name was changed to the Thames Ironworks & Shipbuilding Co. Soon, the new company was bidding for a British Admiralty contract to

An engraving showing part of the inside of the C.J. Mare
& Company shipbuilding works at Blackwall, east
London, c.1854. Note the giant Nasmyth steam hammer
towards the centre of the picture. Mare's Works had
seven of these heavy stamping tools.

HMS Warrior, launched 29 December 1860, was, at the
time, the largest sea-going iron-clad warship in the
world.

HMS Thunderer (22,500 tons), the last major warship
built at the Thames Ironworks, was launched on
1 February 1911.

An engraving showing a general view of the C.J. Mare &
Company shipbuilding works at Blackwall in east
London, c.1854. On the left bank of the waterway is the
Essex yard and on the right bank the Middlesex yard.
The waterway is the River Lea just before it enters the
River Thames. This section of the Lea is known as Bow
Creek.

Bow Creek looking south towards the River Thames as it appears today (1999).

construct what was to become the largest warship afloat, the first sea-going ironclad in the world. HMS *Warrior*, powered by both sail and steam, was launched in December 1860 and was accepted into service by the Royal Navy. Despite being clad with 4 inches(10cm) of iron plate and weighing 9,210 tons, the Warrior could achieve 17½ knots with both power sources engaged.

It is difficult today to imagine that large-scale manufacturing industries such as ironworks and shipbuilding were operating at the southern end of the River Lea. Normally such industries are associated with Scotland, Northern Ireland and north-east England. Between 1840 and 1911 the Thames Ironworks, including 16 years of C.J. Mare, was responsible for the construction of 278 merchant ships.

Perhaps, even more remarkable, the Thames Ironworks, including 10 years of C.J. Mare, built 144 warships. The last to be built at the yard was the 22,500-ton battleship *Thunderer*, which saw service with the Royal Navy during the First World War at the Battle of Jutland.

The Thames Ironworks, in its heyday, ran six departments. These were: marine engines and motor-cars, boatbuilding, cranes, electrical engineering, civil engineering and shipbuilding. During the company's remarkable history it was involved in producing ironwork for a number of diverse civil engineering projects. These included the roof of Alexandra Palace, fabricated sections for Westminster Bridge, Hammersmith Bridge,

I.K. Brunel's Royal Albert Bridge which took the railway over the River Tamar to Saltash in Cornwall. Built in 1859, and still in operation today (1999), with girders supplied by the Thames Ironworks.

Menai Bridge and the construction of gates for Barry Docks in Wales.

Perhaps one of the most spectacular high profile civil engineering projects for which the Thames Ironworks acted as a supplier was Isambard Kingdom Brunel's Royal Albert Bridge (1847-1859), which took the railway over the River Tamar to Saltash in Cornwall. Here 2,650 tons of wrought-iron and 1,200 tons of cast-iron were used. Some of the individual spans weighed in the order of 1,060 tons.

It is therefore quite probable, particularly with the earlier Brunel connection, that the Thames Ironworks could have supplied iron to build the *Great Eastern*. For a ship of the day it was an enormous size, weighing 18,915 tons and being constructed from 30,000 separate iron plates, each held on with 100 rivets. At her launch, in 1858, she was the largest ship afloat, having been designed to carry enough fuel to circumnavigate the globe without stopping. The

Great Eastern was built at John Scott Russell's Millwall yard, only about a mile distant from the Thames Ironworks. This would have made it a simple task for Brunel to discuss his material requirements with the Leamouth yard.

In the latter part of the 19th and early 20th centuries, the Thames Ironworks Shipbuilding & Engineering Co., as it had become known, suffered from a diminishing number of orders from the British Admiralty. Arnold Hills, who had joined the board in 1880, was convinced that the company was experiencing unfair treatment from the Admiralty and he was also of the view that the northern shipyards were operating a price ring. In 1911 Hills petitioned Winston Churchill, then First Lord of the Admiralty, but received little sympathy. December 1912 saw the closure of the Thames Ironworks with the loss of over 70 years' know-how. Viewing the episode from the late 20th century, it does seem curious that government ministers would allow this to happen. With clear indicators of the coming conflict in Europe (the First World War was less than two years away) one would have expected the British Government to have found ways of supporting this talented company with its highly skilled workforce.

Today, in West Ham United Football Club, the memory of the Thames Ironworks lives on. The club's emblem of crossed hammers is a graphic reminder of its Thames Ironworks founding origins.

REFERENCES
Banbury, Philip, *Shipbuilders of the Thames and Medway* (David and Charles, Newton Abbot, 1971)
Falconer, John, *What's Left of Brunel* (Dial House, Surrey, 1995)
Mackrow, G.C., 'Some Reminiscences of the Early Days of the Thames Iron Works and Shipbuilding Company', *Thames Iron Works Gazette*, vol.1 (1895)
Mackrow, G.C., 'Some Reminiscences of the Early Days of the Thames Iron Works and Shipbuilding Company', *Thames Iron Works Gazette*, vol.2 (1896)
Powell, W.R. (ed.), *West Ham 1886-1986* (Council of the London Borough of Newham, 1986)

The Future

IN THIS BOOK we have discussed those past technological achievements which made the Lea Valley the birthplace of the post-industrial revolution. This leads to the question, 'does the region have a future?'.

A number of encouraging indicators to the industrial future of the Lea Valley, which must include the region's social and economic regeneration, allow us to approach the coming millennium with confidence.

Firstly, because of the Lea Valley's diverse industrial base, parts have survived the vagaries of many national and international economic down-turns. Although the manufacturing core has shrunk considerably since the 1950s and early 1960s, the strength of the region has been its industrial diversity. Regions which tend to suffer

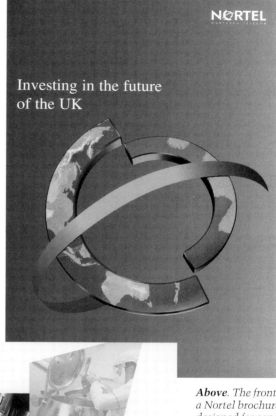

Investing in the future of the UK

Right. A page from a Merck Sharp & Dohme (MSD) brochure which gives a clear commitment to continued investment in Britain. The Company acquired the pharmaceutical firm of Thomas Morson & Son Limited, established in London in 1821, and located at Ponders End, Enfield since 1901. After upgrading, the plant has become MSD's bulk chemical manufacturing facility and is responsible for producing the active ingredients for some of the Company's most important medicines.

BETWEEN 1991 AND 1996 MSD'S INVESTMENT IN UK CAPITAL PROJECTS EXCEEDED £150 MILLION

MSD IN THE UK

Above. The front cover of a Nortel brochure designed for sending a clear message and making a positive commitment to future investment in Britain.

A representative range of transformers built at the Hawker Siddeley Power Transformers plant in Fulbourne Road, Walthamstow in east London.

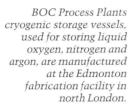

BOC Process Plants cryogenic storage vessels, used for storing liquid oxygen, nitrogen and argon, are manufactured at the Edmonton fabrication facility in north London.

most when global markets decline or technologies change are those which have economies based on a single industrial product, such as coal or iron. Having all the industrial eggs in one basket, once the raw material has been extracted and processed, the community which grew up in support of these industries also dies.

Secondly, the European Union and the UK Government have already recognised that the Lea Valley represents a special case for economic assistance because of the decline of industry. Parts of the region have therefore been granted Objective 2 status. The region has received considerable financial support under the scheme and further funding and assistance are planned for projects which relate to the social and economic regeneration of the community.

Thirdly, in recent years the universities and other educational establishments within the region have recognised the need to introduce new courses and methods of training to serve industry, commerce and the community. A number of partnerships have been formed to assess both the skill requirements of employers and the training needs of the community. Because of changing lifestyles new methods of teaching, as a supplement to traditional methods, are being adopted which address the need for life-long, work-based and distance learning.

Fourthly, support agencies such as the Training Enterprise Councils, Business Link, the Business Innovation Centre and a host of local

Production and assembly of printed circuit board in-car electronic systems at the Ford plant at Ponders End, Enfield for the group's international market.

training bodies have been set up to encourage inward investment, provide assistance to businesses and to bring about the re-skilling of the workforce.

Fifthly, the Lea Valley is served by two of Britain's newest airports, Stansted in the north and London City in the south. Improvements to the region's road and rail networks are taking place and after the proposed development of the channel tunnel high speed rail link, the Lea Valley will have direct and fast access to the markets of Europe.

The modern Johnson Matthey chemical production facility at Brimsdown, Enfield where silver carbonate and other silver salts are manufactured. These materials are used in a wide range of pharmaceutical applications. The Lea Valley family roots of the Company go back to the first half of the 18th century and can be traced to Christopher Johnson, coachman, of Stratford Bow.

Sixthly, major international companies like Ford, Johnson Matthey, Northern Telecom, Hawker Siddeley Power Transformers, Merck Sharp & Dohme and BOC Process Plants, to name but a few, in recent years have invested heavily in the region. This is a powerful indicator by these companies of industrial confidence which will encourage others to invest in the region.

Seventhly, apart from direct connection of the region's waterway, the Lee Navigation, with the River Thames and therefore the docks, the southern end of the Lea Valley is within a short distance of the world's premier financial market—the City of London.

Eighthly, not everything in life is about industry, commerce and work. The region is exceptionally fortunate in having 10,000 acres of parkland running through the valley like a great green artery, managed by the Lee Valley Regional Park Authority. Part of the Authority's mission statement is as follows:

> Our aim is to regenerate, develop, conserve and manage the Lea Valley as a unique leisure resource for the whole community in a way that protects and enhances its environment and sustains it for future generations.

For all the above reasons the Lea Valley is set to have a bright, exciting and prosperous future.

The new Lee Valley Business and Innovation Centre (BIC), located on Rammey Marsh, Enfield, completed autumn 1998.

In Conclusion

THE PURPOSE of this book has been to record and bring together, for the first time in one volume, the unique industrial history of the Lea Valley. There is much left to be done and the author hopes that he has sufficiently inspired others to carry on the research.

To make the book more accessible to a wider readership, the author has deliberately refrained from including too much detail but enough to arouse curiosity. There is plenty of scope for the inquisitive reader to enhance our knowledge of the region through new discoveries. For example, future investigations could include the connections between the following in the Lea Valley:

1. Discoveries in the chemical industry.
2. The manufacture of Parksine and Celluloid.
3. William Friese-Greene and moving pictures.
4. J.A. Prestwich of Tottenham and the manufacture of scientific instruments (began in 1897) and the development of Cinematograph equipment.
5. The film industry in Walthamstow, where several production studios operated during the early part of the 20th century.
6. The Ross Ensign camera company in Walthamstow.
7. The birth of Alfred Hitchcock in Leytonstone.
8. The early Baird experimental television transmissions from Alexandra Palace in the 1930s. Baird used a chemical process for film production prior to the information being transmitted. The process was carried out in studio B.

While it is clear there are connections between some of the happenings, developments and inventions in the above list, there are a few which are not immediately obvious. It will be noted from examples one to eight, although spanning a number of years, all are connected, directly or indirectly, with film and television production. For example, in the development of Celluloid, a material used in early moving pictures, chemicals and chemical processes were used. Could it be that the close proximity of these industries and happenings within the Lea Valley, in some way, influenced or encouraged 'spin-off' developments? Or perhaps there are no connections whatsoever.

'The truth is out there'. Who wants to discover it?

Index

Page numbers given in **bold** indicate illustrations

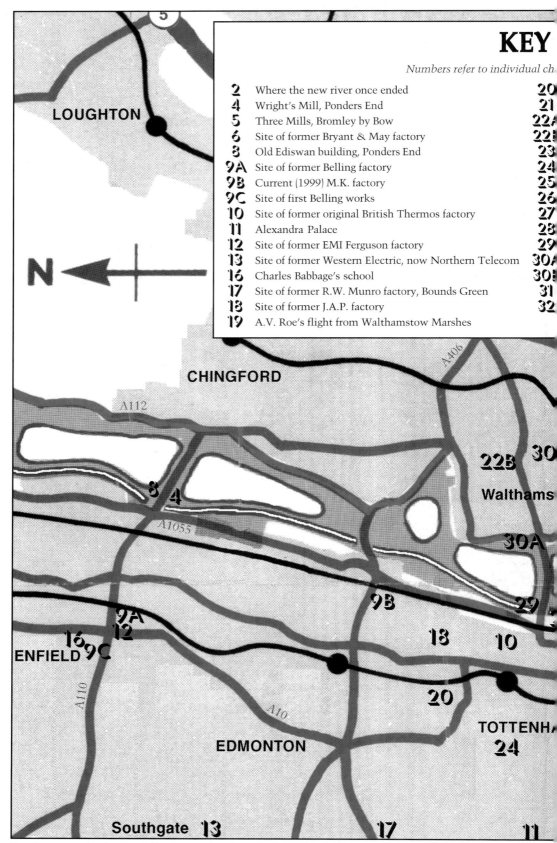

KEY

Numbers refer to individual ch...

2	Where the new river once ended
4	Wright's Mill, Ponders End
5	Three Mills, Bromley by Bow
6	Site of former Bryant & May factory
8	Old Ediswan building, Ponders End
9A	Site of former Belling factory
9B	Current (1999) M.K. factory
9C	Site of first Belling works
10	Site of former original British Thermos factory
11	Alexandra Palace
12	Site of former EMI Ferguson factory
13	Site of former Western Electric, now Northern Telecom
16	Charles Babbage's school
17	Site of former R.W. Munro factory, Bounds Green
18	Site of former J.A.P. factory
19	A.V. Roe's flight from Walthamstow Marshes

20
21
22A
22B
23
24
25
26
27
28
29
30A
30B
31
32

Based on a map by the Lee Valley Regional Park Authority and reproduced with permission